Early Innings

Edited by Scott Bolohan

.406 Press

ISBN 978-1-967135-00-4 (hardcover)
ISBN 978-1-967135-01-1 (paperback)

Front cover image by Mark Mosley.
Book design by Scott Bolohan.

Poetry Editors
Chris Viner
Matthew Johnson

CNF Editors
Joe Hitchcock
Malavika Praseed

Fiction Editors
Bryan St. Amand
Francois Bereaud

First printing, 2025.

.406 Press
3778 Burkoff
Troy, MI 48084

www.406press.com

The Lineup

Letter from the Editor

Illustration by Elliot Lin

Leading Off
By Scott Bolohan

The Twin Bill was born in the early days of the pandemic, when—in a time of fear—I turned to baseball for comfort. Much to my now-wife's displeasure, I decided the best thing to do was watch the entirety of Ken Burns' *Baseball*. I loved hearing all the stories of the history of the game and I wanted to create a place where people could write about baseball and what it meant to them. The only thing stopping me was I had no idea how to do anything like that. Through a lot of trial and error, and probably most importantly through the help of my editors, we were slowly able to create the vision that I had for *The Twin Bill*. What it's become is a surprise to even myself. We built a community.

Now four years later, where does that leave baseball, a sport that's been seemingly on its deathbed from the minute it was born? My response is this anthology. Baseball isn't going anywhere. People are constantly finding new ways to engage with it. It's just morphing, not into your parents' or grandparents' game, but a game of the world. For everyone.

We're in a time of fear again, not just in the United States, but globally. Baseball will not solve these problems. But it's still powerful. It would be easy to think of baseball as a reflection of the time, and you certainly could look at how most Major League teams are actively not trying to win (you could even argue there are 28 or 29 of them) and instead have decided to focus on greed, but that seems cynical. When reading this book, I was struck by how the people who wrote or illustrated these pieces have lived very different lives than me, but we're all baseball fans. And I found that comforting. This book couldn't have happened without the writers, illustrators, editors, and anyone who submitted to or read us. That's a lot of people who were all brought together by baseball.

I hope you enjoy these selections. I'm truly in awe of the talent in these pages. I think it represents everything that we strive to do—to treat every piece as we would want ours to be treated.

I thought the title *Early Innings* was evocative. It's the beginning, when no matter what happens, there's still hope. No one romanticizes early inning home runs, but getting an early lead is so important. Hopefully we've done that.

Scott Bolohan

PS I was looking at a lot of baseball cards when I was making this, and the simple joy of it reading the the litle factoids or trivia questions on the back. So wherever there is room, I added a little trivia question. Enjoy.

Q: Where was The Twin Bill founded?
A: Williamstown, MA, April, 2020

Illustration by Andy Lattimer

Poetry

The Green Monster by William Scherbarth, acrylic and oil pastel on canvas

Fenway Park
By Barbara Varanka

All triangles and memory
signpost green on grass green
on a blue-black night

when the floodlights blind
as you admire the green tower
from Beacon Street and its alleyways

2004 was your confetti frenzy introduction
cheap August bleacher seats
you've worshipped from a hundred angles

learned to keep score at a standing rail
conquered the monster with a hot dog
in hand and avoided a ball to the face

in the front row on opening day
and always that red-orange sign
glowing like a lighthouse

beckoning you back to Kenmore
all triangles and memory

Q: Who is the youngest contributor in *Twin Bill* history?
A: William Scherbarth, six years old

Illustration by Jason David Córdova

Bob From Parkville on The Fan
By Michael Salcman

He calls every talk show from seven A.M. until four.
Must be eighty at least. He's all about the detour.
Argues mostly about sports, sometimes politics,
in a voice which has the soft hush of a respirator,
declaims the greatness of Williams,
(an opinion which I share),
and the evil of Republicans.
Bob recites when each childhood hero first made
a hundred thousand dollars—Ted and Willie, Joe
of the hated Yankees—a sum he himself never got
and how Williams nobly rejected a raise
or bonus towards the end when he hit only 254.
I see Bob wrapped in a shawl, oil lamp lit at his desk,
a portrait of Roosevelt or Melville on the wall.
Imagine the wife's been gone a decade or more
killed off by the endless rant. Bob can't breathe
in empty air so he fills it with ghosts
before the host breaks the connection with a squib:
that was Bob from Parkville (as if none of us knows.)

Q: What piece did Wade Boggs retweet?

A: "What it Takes" by Lillian Marthneau

Illustration by Mark Mosley

The Banishment of Moses Fleetwood Walker
By Matthew Johnson

While waiting for a pitching change
That has grown into a heated debate
Between a frustrated manager and a stubborn pitcher,
Ernie Banks waits in his position,
And grows queasy standing under a pitiless sun for so long.

Careening to his knees from the heat, a man appears to Mr. Cub,
Stretching out a hand to help lift him up.
And like Saul, or Nat Turner, seeing the Son of God,
Ernie Banks sees a dream-like figure,
And it is no other than Moses Fleetwood Walker before him.

The martyr of black baseball, while helping the slugger from the dirt,
Warns the Chicago shortstop to embrace it all, the ups and downs of the sport:
Play two if you must. For I will tell you what they told me at my final game.
You shall not play two. You shall not play one more.
You shall not play today, and you shall not play tomorrow….

Q: When did Matthew Johnson become *The Twin Bill*'s poetry editor?

A: July, 2022

Illustration by Jason David Córdova

Edward Hopper's Nighthawks Consider the 1942 World Series
By Joseph Stanton

"I'm rooting for the Cardinals anyway,"
she mutters staring at her pack of matches.

"No way the Yanks can lose!" he declares
to his wife, the counterman, and the world

in general. "They creamed that Mort Cooper,
and he's the only real pitcher they've got.

This guy Beasley they're putting on the mound
tomorrow? A punk kid. I'll bet the Yankees

chew him up and spit him out in the first.
No way this Series is going more than five."

Q: Who won *The Twin Bill*'s 2023 Best Baseball Poetry Book?

A: Sandra Marchetti, *Aisle 224*

Illustration by Sam Williams

Hitting to the Opposite Field

By Michael Gaspeny

You found the gap almost every at-bat,
lashing clothesline doubles hissing
in the grass between right and center.
Though we edged into your alley,
knowing what was coming,
your blurs whisked our shadows
and sent us running.

I saw you yesterday, twenty years later,
still fit to grip the bat. You caught me up
on your sons: Ted in Kansas, five boys
of his own, so many he could coach
only three of their teams, and Tim
in Minnesota, with a trio of pony-tailed,
softball-playing daughters. I recalled
Ted back in the day, sporting your stroke
and rocket arm, and young Tim, springing
like a terrier around bases between innings.

Sometimes things work out.
The kid doesn't land on the needle
in the sand. The writing on the wall
is a psalm, not a curse. Somehow
the closed stance, inside-out swing,
the liners flicking the green proceed.
God, it was good to see you.

Q: Who has published the most poems in *The Twin Bill*?
A: Michael Gaspeny, five

Illustration by Elliot Lin

The Thrill of Victory, the Agony of Defeat
By Ken Weisner

Michael Yastrzemski, first game, May 25, 2019
            for Allan and Stephen Kuusisto, Red Sox fans
            and Bruce & Nathan Levinson, who were there
1.
In his first major league at-bat, what does Mike do? Digs in like he belongs, grandson
        of hall-of-famer Carl,
takes a couple called strikes, lays off a close one, spoils another, then shazaam! a
        bloop hit,
a dying quail to left and the crowd goes nuts. We're witnessing history. Or what
        passes for it in baseball.

Immediately we're on our feet and Mike, wide-eyed, stoked, aggressive, flying,
rounds first base right in front of us, everyone's hands raised—
we're watching his arrival, his first big-league hit.

This has been a bad year for the home team, and a very bad game as well, pretty
much over by the second inning. Mike is the new call-up,
blessed and saddled with his name—the glory of his grandfather.

*

So here's what happens. Mike rounds first base a step too far—just a single step—
a little adrenaline-fueled bravado, maybe to see if the left fielder juggles it—after all,
that's how you play the game; he's 28, still a youngster, but old for a rookie.

Snake Swihart sees that extra step, short hops the ball in shallow left,
pumps a bullet behind Mike straight toward us so Yaz has to put on the breaks,
a blur of spinning cartoon legs now in reverse, a scramble, then a headfirst dive
        back to the bag,

but Swihart's throw is a clothesline, on the money, and baby-faced Mike
is hung out, dead in the water, his dying quail, now a dead duck—
you're OUT! howls the umpire, turns his back, walks decisively. Welcome to the
        big leagues kid.

*

Michael's wife and family, even his mother, all in the stands, their joy even greater
        than ours
now heads-in-hands, groan—Mike has to stand up, dust himself off,
head back to the dugout where teammates will kindly, grimly, avert their eyes

while the Snakes tamp down their own guffaws,
still obliged to throw the ball back to the dugout for safekeeping,
the traditional trophy for a first big-league hit, like saving the corsage.

You keep it. On your mantle, in your trophy case. It's for the ecstatic memory,
to keep the inner-movie of the special moment alive, forever.

But in this case, file it under comedy, Buster Keaton, the groom forgot the rings.

2.
So… actually Mike has a great game after that, two more hits and ever since,
a wonderful late-blossoming career. But what we're left with from that day
is the five-part operatic sequence, squeezed into those ten seconds:

Yes, yes, yes, yes!
        no! no! no! no! —
oh my God, oh my God, oh my God—

This this this… is the funniest thing I've ever seen—
        Don't laugh, don't laugh. I said don't laugh.
Such dignity! Be nice to the boy, stand, give a round of applause.

*

The human face & body can register all of these expressions
within a ten-second period. In a game so famous for humiliation,
this one was too good to be true, and those seats, just that once, right by first base.

For Mike, the mythic joy. The latent dream, realized. The brutal reversal, quick as a snake.
The initiation. The holding his head high.
No, we are not people to relish other people's misfortune.

We are sympathetic to those who can never live up
to the expectations, the name. The hall-of-famer's grandson failed magnificently,
held his head high and won our hearts. We loved him now.

*

So much comedy here! Of his name, impossible to spell.
Of the grandfather he can never remotely live up to.
Of his very late blooming.

Of his learning the hard way before all those eyes,
packed stadium, live TV. But let's also be very clear
about one thing. Mike's not dead. He didn't take one step too far

from the curb—or the foxhole. Not mowed down
by a machine gun or a bus. It's game day
vs. the Snakes, an operatic form.

Or consider the comedy of telling the story of that moment
forever, no matter your subsequent triumphs, of being roasted for it perpetually
by the people who love you.

3.
I do love writing the "Z" in his name. The core letter, the anchor
of the five on either side. A whole sports team of letters.
Zed at the core. You're a true leader, Zed. You died out there.

Jastrząbki, a town of fifty people. In the district of Olsztyn,

They say one of the happiest places in Poland, traded over centuries
from the Teutonic Germans to the Russians to the Nazis to the Poles.

Michał Jastrzębski and Teofila Suchcicka , Josephine Mierzejewska ,
Michael Skonieczny , Eva K. Mezynieski.
I wonder if your grandfather felt he could ever live up to them.

Jastrzębski, a Polish name, from *Jastrząb*, hawk.
I see now it is the 2,789,887th most common surname of all.
And yet just as glorious as the name of any man, named after any bird.

*

NOTE: Carl Yastrzemski: (born 1939) US baseball player; known as Yaz; full name Carl
Michael Yastrzemski. With the Boston Red Sox from 1961 until 1983, he had 452 career home
runs and 3,419 career hits. Baseball Hall of Fame (1989). In his first full year, 2020, Mike
Yastrzemski was 12th in OPS in all of major league baseball and has established himself as a
front-line major league baseball talent.

Q: How many illustrations has *The Twin Bill* published in their first 16 issues?

A: 150

Illustration by Jason David Córdova

How to Spit in Little League Baseball
By Karen J. Weyant

Too young for tobacco, they chew gum or suck
on hard butterscotch candy. Sometimes,

they just resort to old fashioned phlegm,
snorting, gurgling in back of their throats, until

they have worked up a wad professional players
would be proud of. But mostly they love

sunflower seeds that come in all flavors:
Dill pickle, Chili Pepper, Jalapeno Hot Salsa.

They suck on them, learn to crack them open
with their teeth, pull the seeds from their hulls, spit

so that dugouts, base lines and outfields are littered
with shells. They trade flavors, rate their favorites.

There are only a few rules. Never spit at each other.
Never spit at the opposing team players.

Never spit at a coach. And never, ever spit at the umpires.
Even when you hate what they have to say.

Q: Who has illustrated the most pieces in *Early Innings*?

A: Jason David Córdova, 16

Illustration by Jason David Córdova

The Old Ball Game

By Kenny Likis

I dig in, squeeze the bat, spit
I look the pitcher in the eye and mouth
I am going to undress you
The pitcher snickers, lets it fly
But I am sitting in a red collapsible camping chair
on the shore of Walden Pond reading
a poem that never strikes out
letting the game come to me
The poem stirs memories thicker than jambalaya
The poem leads the league in extra-base hits
Up the shore Henry David Thoreau is bathing
his skin so white you'd think he descended from Easter lilies
so white you'd think his parents poured him from a milk bottle
Henry David brags he's a switch-hitting shortstop
I listen to his chatter, wade out and dive in
I practice my backstroke I float like baby Moses
Next time up I walk on four straight pitches
I scoot to first and get back to reading my poem

Q: What is the most-read poem in *Twin Bill* history?

A: "The Old Ball Game" by Kenny Likis

Illustration by Michaela Paulson

the iguana is a huge baseball fan

By Brendan Walsh

it's the best thing you people ever did,
he bounces his head up&down the way
iguanas do when they're swallowing
or just really happy. he watches games

through the windows of the Dominican
family across the street, perched on low
royal poinciana branches, his couch.
he's mesmerized by the stillness, then *bam,*

they swing, throw, run. it's like something scares them.
the grass looks nice, too. i could lay for hours
in left field and no one would realize.
he's loves the marlins, but it's all the same

who wins or loses. it's still sun and field.

Q: What animal was featured in the first piece published in *The Twin Bill*?

A: Scott Bolohan's dog, Annie.

Illustration by Jason David Córdova

Charro Jacket

By Christopher Rubio-Goldsmith

When the Dodgers won the World Series
Joe Kelly wore a charro jacket to el White house,
Olvidate. His big glasses just
adding to his all-American look.
Pero sabes que his madre is puro Riverside.

Ted Williams would never have owned
a Charro jacket, even though his mom cleaned
rooms and made tortillas by hand. His homers
must have been rockets of internal oppression.

I wonder if this went down at Joe's high school
while sitting in a dugout on a bright So Cal afternoon,
Joe needed to check his white teammates
when they said something about "all the illegals" in the
classes. And later when they imitated
the mispronunciation of words "school"
becoming "eschool," "ship" evolving into "sheep"
this of course signaling to them, the dugout crowd,
the destruction of Western Civilization, the goats arriving
before the priests. An existing social order
that felt like a fastball hit off a splintering bat
resulting in an easy fly ball for the second baseman.

What did it feel like to put that charro jacket
onto his torso in the Capitol? That fabric cut with lines
like the banks of that arroyo in every barrio. The jacket
a classic fit, created over time and by seasonal
flowing waters that ran on and off when the land
was not this place of baseball. And later the
arroyo shaping itself to the world it moves into, infuses,
adapts slowly but still vines into sharp lines
through the valley that provides for the indifferent fields.

Who doesn't like the charro jacket? It is the
sound of horns before the sound of horns.
It is Chavela Vargas wearing it as she sings
La Llorona, danger, damage, desire all
blessed under the buttons. The charro jacket
is the story of celebration or the story of struggle or both.

Q: Who won *The Twin Bill*'s 2024 Best Baseball Poetry Book?
A: *Pretend the Ball is Named Jim Crow* by Dorian Hairston

Illustration by Jason David Córdova

Two Memories of Miguel Cabrera Two-Run Homers
By Matt Gulley

The key to longevity is to learn every aspect of music that you can – Prince

the first memory of two, comes in a haze
I was mostly drunk and alone those days

on a beat-up couch, leaning perilously forward
in Ferndale, Michigan,
August 9th, 2013

watching baseball and convincing myself
my life was full of the stuff that mattered

key interests, a good and demanding job
but it was television keeping me company

Mariano Rivera, enter sandman
on a grand retirement tour

sought to face down Miggy,
a hobbled giant on a single leg

the color commentary sang the choir
the greatest ever vs. the great of his era

and the coronation hit a hiccup
Cabrera smashed it out to tie the game

something I could text to friends
with exclamation points, and wait for reply
they would not come, I had drove them away

time leaps forward, I was
living another life it seemed

sober and content,
"the fear" put away in a hole, shoveled over

in Detroit, my home, but visiting from somewhere else
with my family, my partner, and the sun
September 12th, 2021

and here comes the man, the big man
nearing a decade past his prime, like me

and there were no high stakes
another miserable season in the books

but he came to the plate, all regardless
he still had a job, like me

and each time, the crowd leaned perilously forward
the communal sway of spectators as sunflowers

three at-bats had come and gone
strike-out, ground-out, and struck-out again

and these games, these days
they go on long, don't they?

and here he comes again,
still commanding the fingers to grip

the bat of his, that heavy wand
and all the fingers on cups and seats

and smash again, out of the park
beyond the wall, to raise the squall

we all went home happy
I always used to go home scared

and today, *April 23rd, 2022*
I am moved to write about these feats

because the man, the big man Miggy
has hit a ball three thousand times

and ever-the-journalist, I fact-check myself
only to find, on that day in September

he hadn't gone long at all,
just a well-placed single to advance two men

but what had happened that day,
was less about the true facts stated

and like all of sports, and all endeavor
was about what I chose instead to remember

because it tells a better story
about where I was and where I am

so thank you, Miguel Cabrera,
and out of great love, and respect,

I will not be changing the title
of this piece, because to me

most important of all,
it remains the truth, and always will be thus –

Q: What former Detroit Tiger was on *The Twin Bill* podcast?
A: Lance Parrish, Episode 13

"Meet the" Vignettes

Matt Gulley

Who are you?

I'm a resident of Fort Greene, a neighborhood in Brooklyn, NY, where I live with my wife Jenna. I make a living as an underwriter and write poetry, fiction, and the occasional play. I had writerly aspirations as a teenager and then put those aside for a long time, getting serious about writing again in 2022, funnily enough after watching the movie *Tick Tick Boom*. It's not even a movie I would say is a personal favorite, but there was something about it that made me want to kick my own ass.

What was the inspiration for your piece?

The reasoning for writing the piece is explained in the poem itself, which can happen—sometimes a piece of art is about itself. I'd seen a headline that Miguel Cabrera, the Tigers great, had reached the 3000-hit milestone. I reflected on two particular memories of Miguel Cabrera hitting home runs, only to find out when reading the box scores for research that the second memory I had was false, he hadn't actually hit a home run in that game. The realization that I'd invented a memory was interesting, as was the fact that I was a miserable drunk in the first memory and a happier sober person in the second.

What's your favorite team?

Detroit is a four-sport town, so will always have sentimentality towards the Tigers, Lions, Pistons, and Red Wings. The Jim Leyland-era Tigers were a special group, with Cabrera, Prince Fielder, Max Scherzer, and Justin Verlander on the roster, to name a few. Second favorite baseball team is the Mets, which is my wife's favorite team.

Who is your favorite player?

Probably Cabrera.

What's your favorite baseball memory?

Not my favorite, but the funniest was going to a minor-league game in Chicago when I was a teenager and a batter got hit by a pitch and fell to the ground in pain, which was not at all funny, but what was extremely funny was when they almost immediately started playing the ER theme song over the sound systems. It was a mix of the inappropriate levity and the fact that they had this sound cue at the ready. I'll never forget it.

What's the highlight of your writing career?

So far, so good—being included in this anthology is certainly something I'm proud of. Working with the fiction editor of Consequence Forum on a short story of mine they published was also a highlight, just the attention and care they had for making the piece better was something I'd like to be a part of more often.

Favorite baseball writer?

Anything from Jon Bois.

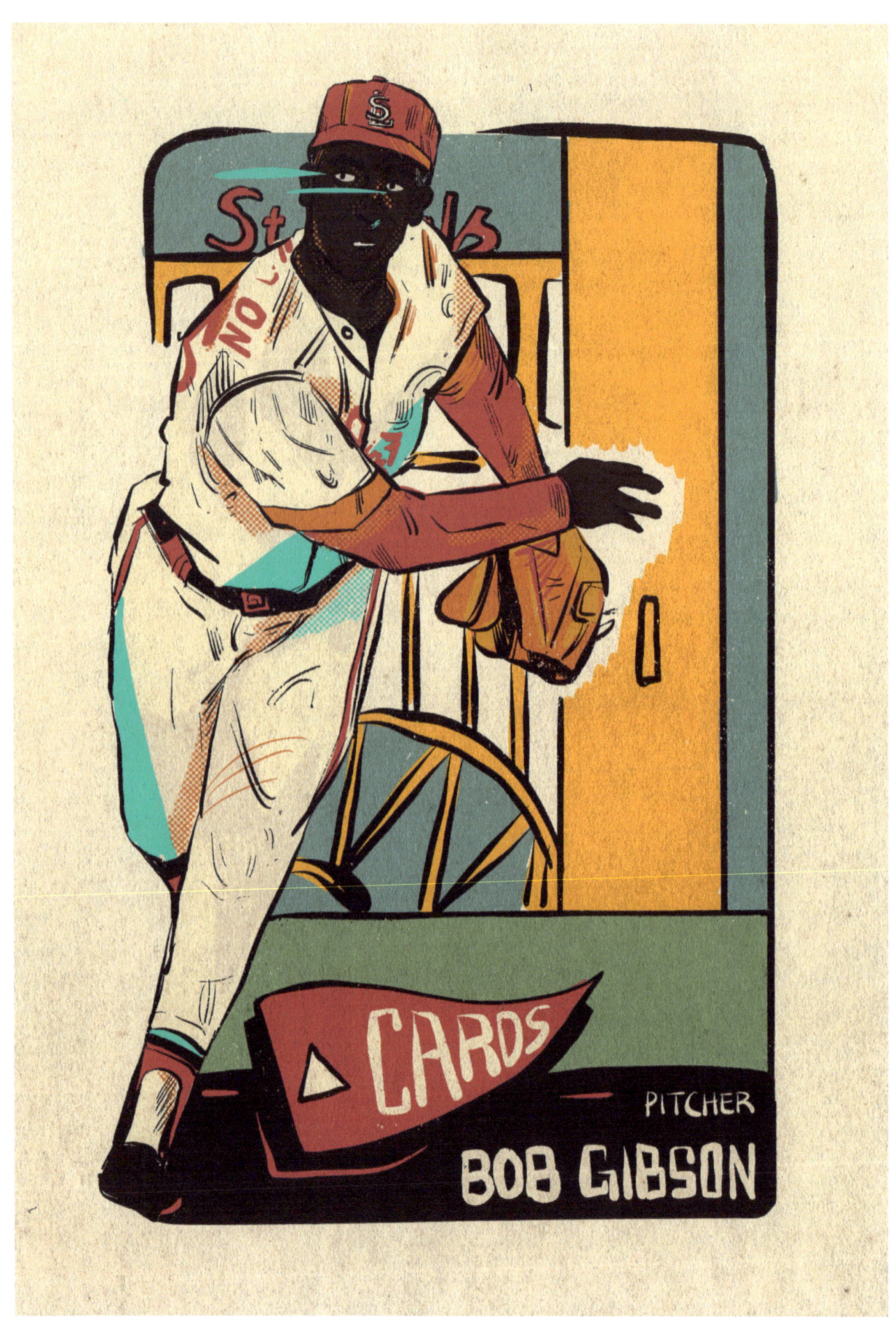

Illustration by Elliot Lin

"I'm Pitching Today"

By Robert Stewart

I was committed to his heart.
        —Mgr. Johnny Keane,
                on Bob Gibson

Bob Gibson had to say
        that sentence twice,
"I'm pitching today,"
        to Lou Brock
before the second game,
        when Brock just
wanted to tell him a joke.
        A joke. Nothing
was a joke to Gibson.

Q: Interviewed in Issue Nine, what player faced Bob Gibson in the 1968 World Series?

A: Willie Horton

Illustration by Jason David Córdova

Captain Dynamite Will Blow Himself Up

By Amanda Kooser

Patrick "Midnight" O'Brien doffed
his merchant marine hat
with the eagle crest, wings raised
surrounded by laurels

he gave his crown
to the groundskeeper
strapped his craggy head
into a gold helmet sparkling
in the early evening sun
and laid face down
in his paper coffin of death

we came for the game, yes
for the Arkansas Travelers
for the molasses sweetness
of Cracker Jacks in June

but we came also
for Captain Dynamite
for the spectacle of sparks
the pop of explosives
ringing across the field

in those moments of suspense
the smoke dissipated like clouds
the man lay motionless, prone
every bit as compelling
as a full count awaiting the pitch

a stadium held its breath
until he rose to the kind
of applause usually reserved
for home run kings
such daring, such madness
he lingers as a shadow of myth
in our minor league memories

Q: Who has done the most illustrations in *Twin Bill* history?

A: Jason David Córdova, 52

Illustration by Sam Williams

Baseball Haiku
By Richard Jordan

fastball
clanks off the backstop—
ice cream truck

record heat
even a pop fly
to center takes it slow

nursing home
on good days grandpa curses
Bucky Bleeping Dent

kids in the bleachers
resurrect a wave—
down to the final out

Q: The Twin Bill sponsors which UK baseball team?

A: New Forest Thunder Knights

Illustration by Elliot Lin

The Day that Baseball Taught Third Grade

after Brad Aaron Modlin
By Robert Fillman

Mr. Ripken explained how perfect attendance
is about more than just showing up. During

morning announcements, Mr. Kalas crackled
a warm horsehide good luck to the Chess Club

before their match against their better-funded
powerhouse division rivals. In Language Arts,

Mr. Weaver diagrammed extravagant sentences
with his arms that made perfect sense to students

despite their only knowing a few four-letter words.
Mr. DiMaggio explained how not to squirm

in your seat, how 56 could be considered
a prime number. Mr. Williams worked with students

at their desks on fractions, going over a worksheet
where every answer somehow came out to .406.

After lunch, Mr. McGraw talked about spirituality,
responded to every persistent question about faith

by saying, "You Gotta Believe." For art class,
Mr. Maddux demonstrated how to paint

corners, how to create visual movement in pictures
using the slightest touch of a finger. Then

everyone stretched. The afternoon history lesson
was led by Mr. Robinson, who managed to integrate

CRT without ever uttering terms like discrimination
or privilege, instead passing around bottles and rocks

and rope as props. Realizing the afternoon bell
was about to ring, Mr. Buckner closed the day

by gathering everyone around him. He told the class
everyone makes mistakes, that everyone will be

remembered for something, so strive to be good,
above all else, always strive to be good.

Illustration by Mark Mosley

Munson

By Loren Broaddus

There is a photograph
of Munson celebrating
the Chambliss walk-off
to win the '76 American
League pennant.
As a kid, I hated that moment,
my Royals heartbreakingly
defeated by the swashbuckling
Yankees, Munson, the Captain,
not loved at my house
back in that bicentennial
autumn, although later
I remember hearing
of his Ohio plane crash and crying,
all our swashbuckling
momentarily broken.

Q: Who has illustrated the most covers for *The Twin Bill*?

A: Mark Mosley, three

Illustration by Mark Mosley

Spitballing in the Writing Center

By Tim Peeler

He was an earnest late teenager
With a big friendly grin, dark-haired,
Chubby-faced, a fuzzy half beard,
Ball cap, jeans, a solid looking kid,
Come for help on a project
For this developmental English class.
It was a narrative with pictures,
The aim of which was to show
Appreciation to someone they admired.
I looked at the big old guy in the photos,
His grandpa, a grizzled mountain farmer
In Spruce Pine who loved his family.
Though he'd lost his wife, he went on,
Had been a ballplayer and a coach
A long time ago, picture after picture,
I saw a face I should recognize till
I finally asked him Who is your grandpa?
Gaylord Perry, he said, flat and
Matter of factly as a McDonald's order.
300-win club Gaylord Perry.
Me and the Spitter, Gaylord Perry.
Named after a friend of his Daddy's
Who died having his teeth pulled.
Cy Young in both leagues, Gaylord Perry.
Campaigned for Jesse Helms, Gaylord Perry.
Don't you think we ought to mention
The baseball a little more? I asked,
And he looked at me like I didn't know nothing.
Shifting in his chair, he said,
That's just my granddaddy.

Q: How many poems did The Twin Bill publish over their first 16 issues?

A: 117

Illustration by Jason David Córdova

Myron Noodleman Has a Bad Day

By Genoa Wilson

It's not as easy as it looks, you know.
Winters spent ratcheting up a touring schedule
fielding offers from cheapskate minor league teams.
What the hell am I doing?

Come summer on the road, I stay in motels
out on the highway.
I know the inside of most minor league ballparks better
than I know my own soul.

Problem is, no one wants to give me big bucks for this and I have
kids in college and a wife
who asks me why on earth would I leave
a job teaching math to spend
Friday nights and sticky Sunday afternoons
prancing around the bleachers and dancing like a dang fool
on top of a dugout.

She comes to the Tulsa Drillers game when I'm there
her church group spelled out on the scoreboard in lights.
I can see her duck her head when I point at her.
The cheap hot dog and beer fans laugh.
A small child throws up on my shoe.

Q: What award was this poem nominated for?

A: Best of the Net

Illustration by Jason David Córdova

The Meaning of Life According to a Groundskeeper
By Ethan Altshul

In the newly-white dirt he finds himself
a player, or as close to a player as his body
will allow him. The grass, as he mows it,

is marred by inconsistency—some sod
risen above sod. What does that
feel like? It doesn't matter. He cuts

it down. What does *that* feel like? Doesn't
matter, it's all even now for the kids, well
really the players, to enjoy it, to orbit

like great bodies of celestial gas, ready
for Jupiter at third pulling the boos and cheers
into its ellipse. Ready for the crack

of the seam-woven solar flare to draw
it away over the fresh foul lines. He's sure
that'd make some grass taller. Really,

what does that feel like? Still doesn't
matter. Just matter for antimatter. Just
some raked vacuum in the Milky Way.

At least, that's what a Groundskeeper says.

Q: Who was the youngest poet published by *The Twin Bill*?

A: Ethan Altshul, 17

Illustration by Sam Williams

You're Out

By Lawrence Miles

I misread the no smoking sign on the bus
And thought it stood for
No baseball bats allowed on the bus

I've never tried to take a baseball bat on the bus
But I would doubt if the bus driver would stop me
As long as I did not look like I would use it on the bus

If I was wearing a baseball uniform
It would be easier to pull off
And if it was the uniform of a major league team
Complete with pants
Which you rarely see on a fan
I might even get a few curious looks
From people mistaking me for a Triple-A prospect
Called up for a season-ending cup of coffee

Maybe they would even ask me for an autograph
And I would gladly give it
Because it would be rude not to.

Q: Which issue published the most poems?

A: Issue Eight, 11

Illustration by Jeff Brain

INTERVIEW WITH MY ROTATOR CUFF

By AJ Speier-Wallace

there are twenty one muscles in the shoulder,
or so the ortho tells me. you need all of them to pitch.
you can do almost anything with a shoulder: up/down/right/left— the possibilities are endless
our bodies were made to do almost anything with this joint except overhand throwing. there is nothing
in the world as explosive, and so we do it anyway,
like the creation of airplanes or micro plastics, human curiosity has always spanned domains over
which we have no right.
and so we go one hundred and five miles per hour over sixty feet and six inches. we shouldn't; it will
kill us at least twice.
with the same ferocity as every idiot who came before me, I let myself fall in love
I am not the first boy to break in a glove.
when the spot between my collarbone and my neck starts to pull I am handed a pop quiz on material I
was beginning to understand:
which of the following is true?
a)   your arm is everything you have
b)   your arm is everything you have
c)   your arm is everything you have
d)   your arm is everything you have
the answer is not only e, all of the above, but for extra credit:
your trinity of heroes is your shoulder, your elbow, and your wrist, each one worth double its weight
in gold
every single one will betray you, whether sooner or later. this is the first thing to learn about your body
the second, of course, will be your perpetual mantra: your arm is everything you have

Q: Which awards was this poem nominated for?
A: Pushcart Prize and Best Small Fictions

Illustration by Jason David Córdova

The phanatic
By Tim Livingston

I want to make a garden of my heart
        A mossybacked creature

It's been that way before
        Every time he hits a home run
        the auteur, the tyrant   I have two of me at least
and we're reminded of the time
he hit a home run

        The sweaty throbbing
        ball of light in the bleachers
        of becoming   screaming
        hoarsely   reminding us
                to feed it

One the seed two the shade
three the root four the rain

I want to make a garden of my heart
It never tells me what to be   but it's alive! At best
I don't watch it grow but I feel it
        I think

        It grows like a body
                truthfully

When it echoes
        when it's empty   when it's getting faint
        it's getting faint again

what else can we do?

One the seed two the shade
three the root four the rain

I want to make a garden of my heart
I can't be so flexible that a tumble feels like flying
        that to drown feels elegant, all alone

                alone as a sunset

                but I can consider dancing
        dancing
dancing on dugouts

What a glory then
        a lifelong project

it's made of me!
For the people!
For the people!

One the seed two the shade
three the root four the rain

Illustration by Sam Williams

The Pursuit of Affirmation Begins, Shea Stadium, 1987
By Susie Aybar

I wear a belted mock turtleneck
bloused over white parachute pants
hair moussed, bangs scrunched

"The Lady in Red" blares on the PA
at Shea, we buy warm, salty pretzels
Cracker Jacks with peanuts

We pull apart powder-blue cotton candy
as Keith Hernandez rounds first
clouds of puppy love, sticky and sweet

We watch the '87 Mets
I think they win
we ride home in the back of the dark blue Delta 88

The staticky AM station, a soundtrack
the only interference between us
and my parents in the front seat

When we scooch closer
my pants bunch from the velour bench seat
radio news crackles and hisses

His clammy hand reaches for mine
under the jean jacket between us
our faces meet underneath it

Remnants of pretzel and mustard linger
when his mouth opens
I feel the hard metal of braces

When we emerge, the headlights shine on us
awkward glances, auburn hair, freckled cheeks
in the black of the back seat, we'd been invisible

I see him years later, his hair faded red, beard speckled white
I smell the malty pretzel, hear the radio hiss
feel the plush darkness, first kiss

Q: Who was the first guest on *The Twin Bill* podcast?
A: Joe Berton, the real-life Sidd Finch

Illustration by Jason David Córdova

Braves at Phillies, 10/14/22
By Jared Frank

full crowd crying their verdict at the
visiting batter, and his offseason crime

(*DUI, DUI, DUI*),

and you're offering me candy, Ziploc laden
with gum and Jolly Ranchers, yes, I'll take one

and you say your son told you *who brings candy
to a baseball game,* he's as stone-faced next

to you as the batter hearing
spiteful ball hitting catcher's mitt

but we're smiling as the green
apple gum dissolves to paste

on my tongue, Fall afternoon melting
to evening, jeers melting to clamor melting to buzz.

Q: What Philadelphia sandlot team does *The Twin Bill* sponsor?
A: Quaker City Crypôds

Illustration by Jason David Córdova

BART

By Jack Albert

He chain-smoked his way
throughout every lecture
while pitching the essence
of the Divine Comedy—

From the depths of purgatory
to the green fields of summer,
he juxtaposed literary images
with baseball analogies.

No surprise when the professor
was named commissioner,
giving the game ultimate
class and stature—Dr. Giamatti,
most fluent and learned fan—

And when Pistol was caught
gambling on his team—
Bart stood tall defending the
honor code, reminding us all
of the grand unwritten rule.

I'll always remember the cigarettes
dangling from his sturdy hand,
one after another until the lecture ended.
Only five months on the job, age 51,
Bart went to bat for the soul of the game,
puffing away into baseball heaven.

Q: Which Pete Rose biographer was on *The Twin Bill* podcast?
A: Keith O'Brien, Episode 3

Illustration by Jason David Córdova

Grave of the Cracker Jack Boy
By Cynthia Gallaher

Robert Muno Rueckheim (aka "Sailor Jack") 1913-1920
(buried at St. Henry Catholic Cemetery at Devon & Ridge, Chicago)

"Buy me some peanuts and cracker jack,
I don't care if I never get back."
                ~ "Take Me Out to the Ball Game"

Sailor boy, sailor boy,
at age three you posed
as Sailor Jack
holding tight to stray dog Bingo
on the box of Cracker Jack.

Grandson of the man who
launched his candy-glazed
popcorn and peanut snack
at the 1893 World's Fair
in Chicago.

Which amniotic seas did you travel
to arrive at our inland harbor, getting sea legs
enough to stand astride like a real sailor
to give a high-sign salute,
only to succumb to pneumonia at age seven,

A too-early watery ending,
our hope that when you entered death
you found a prize inside,
or at least reunite with the others,
the Morton Salt girl, Campbell Soup kids,
Coppertone child and Gerber baby.

Yet one hundred years later,
ever young still,
you self-fulfill many a child's fantasy
at every baseball game,
to be rooting from the stands.

Q: Which episode of The Twin Bill Podcast did Cynthia Gallaher read this poem on?
A: Episode Five

Illustration by Elliot Lin

Ruth Talks Hitting

By Dana Yost

It's a young Ruth, slimmer,
certainly not the caricatured
fat man. He's wearing a Yankees
uniform, pinstriped but with no
logo, except for the overlaid *NY* on the cap.
He's showing a man in a suit
and fedora something with his bat,
cradling it near the trademark,
as if to say this is the sweet spot,
where I hit them the best, the
farthest. The man in the fedora
— maybe a New York sports writer —
looks on intently, but with a slight
smile — perhaps picturing one
of Ruth's majestic clouts
into the far reaches of the Stadium.
They're in front of the Yankees dugout,
probably pre-game, and I wish
I had been there, eavesdropping,
or even in the midst of the conversation,
listening in as greatness explains
what it means, what it *takes*,
to be great. How it feels to become legendary.
Did Ruth hit a homer
later, in that game, the one
in the photograph — did he find
the sweet spot that day?
I want to say yes, I want to say
that he slugged one beyond
the limit of sight, the ball falling
like a rocket, landing with a racket
— so loud, oh God, *so* loud —
in the seats, or maybe deeper,
rattling around an outfield concourse.
I want to say that's how it happened.
I want to say Ruth was Ruth and the bat
was sweet and so was the swing —
and so was the swing, then and forever.

Q: What team does Editor-in-Chief Scott Bolohan give tours for?

A: New York Yankees

Illustration by Sam Williams

Men's league ballplayer

By Nick Visconti

Beneath his hat his hair ebbs
though it spills down his neck

like a subtle lie. The ligaments
holding him together wheeze

and pop, taking after his lungs,
beaten to hell by smoke-breaks

between innings. He still lays out
in the gravel-strewn outfield,

bottlecaps and rocks, these days.
Shoulders frozen, hips, locked,

destined for replacement. If he
were to retire, who would he be?

Why does his family, once a main-
stay down the foul line, stay home?

Q: What UK baseball team does Issue 4 contributor Aaron M. Kahn manage?

A: Oxford Kings

Illustration by Michael C. Paul

Night Game: April 8, 2024

By James Scruton

Night games were played in several Major League cities
*   along the "totality" path of that afternoon's solar eclipse.*

By game time the sky was once more
ordinary, that big moon just another
hanging curve, stadium lights blazing
in their familiar constellations.

Had the game been earlier we might've seen
our first day-night single-header,
everyone with protective eyewear,
some outfielder losing a fly ball in the non-sun.
We'd have called each homer a moonshot,
watched pitchers throw lights-out stuff.

Instead we'll remember how,
when the heavens swung, we missed
our chance. We'll find an E for error
in the cosmic box score, tell ourselves
there's always next solar year

Q: What is another name for a 'twin bill?'

A: Double header

Illustration by Elliot Lin

Creative Nonfiction

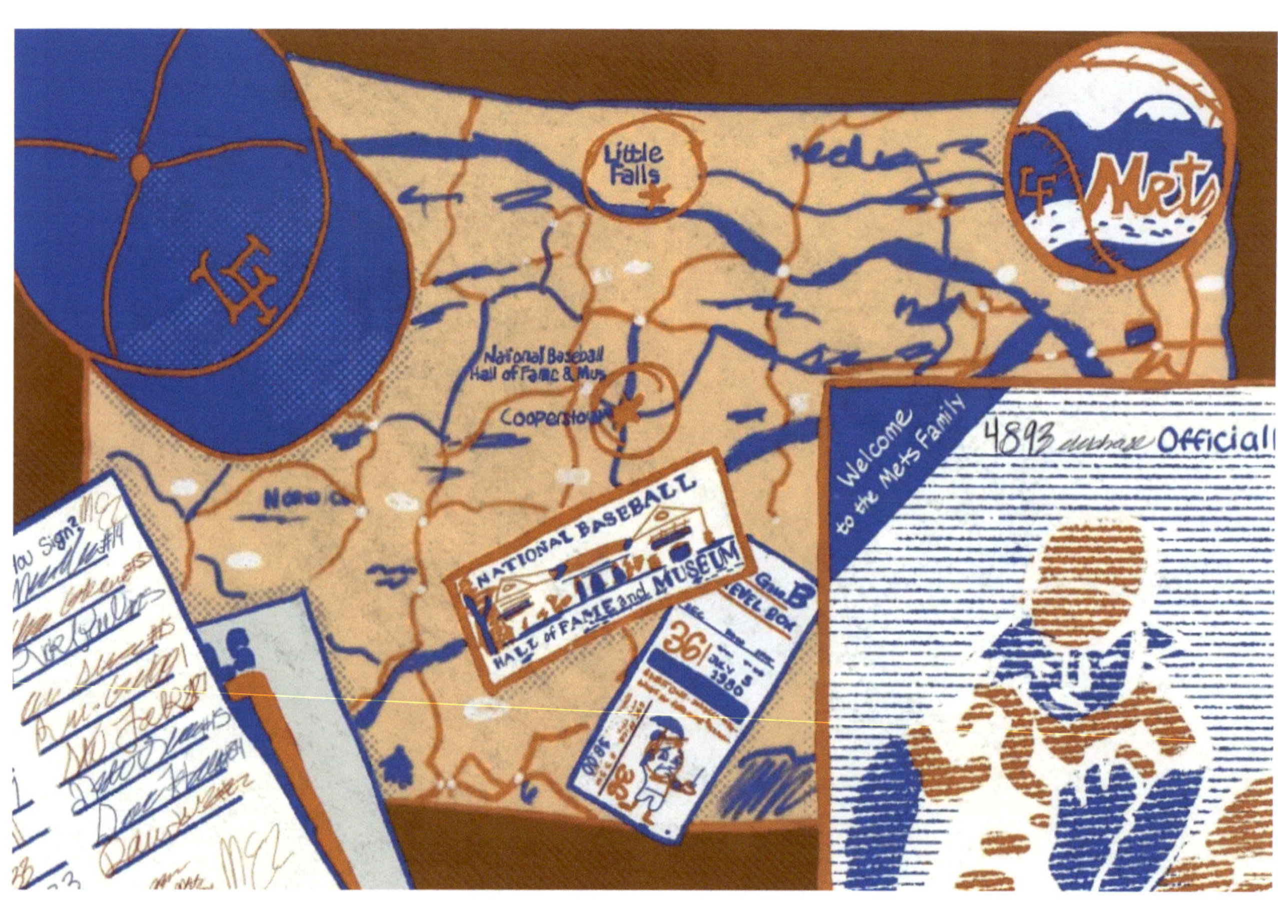

Illustration by Andy Lattimer

The Road to Cooperstown
By Mike Cecconi

When I was a young boy, the only thing I found interesting about my hometown of Little Falls, NY, was that we had an affiliated minor league baseball team, the smallest city to have one. It was the lowest affiliate of the New York Mets, in the New York-Penn League, for teenagers drafted straight out of high school.

Most of them, of course, wouldn't make the big time but just a few of them in five years would be millionaires playing on WWOR, near Young People's Day Camp—no doubt feasting on Goya and Fudgie The Whales—in the terrifying miracle, New York City. A four-hour drive a world away, but for one summer they had to live in the place I tried to escape with books and TV—a momentary distraction on the road to fortune and fame. That's how I saw my childhood as well, back then.

They moved when I was nine. First to Pittsfield, then finally to Brooklyn, so unfairly close to the goal of all dreamers. Maybe starting out at the edges of greatness isn't a good idea, maybe time down in the sticks running on nothing but hope pushes you harder. Maybe distance makes it matter. Most of them never made it, either way. I went broke in Brooklyn once myself.

For the great, the road to Cooperstown's paved with 500 home runs. Where I grew up, the road to Cooperstown's paved with 500 speed traps on Route 28, every cop for 30 miles slavering to nail reckless tourists with the tickets to pay their mortgages.

When I was a teenager, someone rummaged through the defunct team's old office and found a roll of tickets for the Little Falls Mets. I bought a few to hold as keepsakes. I collect all kinds of souvenirs from that team thirty years gone, pennants, programs—all the ephemera minor-league teams generate. I save them as physical proof it all actually happened. It all seems so impossible, seems so far away, those young men striving for greatness, my own dreams. But the tickets held a special magic for me. I wore them in hospital bands for surgeries, sacrificed them after teenage heartbreaks over girls who could only love boys who play guitar, until I eventually only had one of them left to my name.

In my twenties, I went back to the Cooperstown Hall, past the speed traps, but there was no mention of my Little Falls Mets. A footnote, at best, thirty-odd years ago, now beneath history's notice entirely. In this life, though, we take our lumps and learn the little ways to make marks, nonetheless. I folded up that last ticket, tucked it behind the frame of some random exhibit. If you happen to see a fleck of blue somewhere in the frames, maybe it's even still there. At the fringe, my Little Falls Mets enshrined in the Hall of Fame despite all sane reasons to the contrary.

And in some even tinier, more secret way? Maybe that starstruck yearning little boy too.

Q: Which Met played in the most games in franchise history and was interviewed in Issue 13?

A: Ed Kranepool

Illustration by Tanya Ramsey

Let's All Get Up
By Carey Bowman

There are little moments that kids remember, moments that seem insignificant to their parents. When we would go hiking, I could never make it to the top, being heavyset and all. Over time, though, I strengthened up, and instead of asking my dad to carry me to the top (an act that, I think, limited the number of hikes we went on), I made it all the way to the crest—I conquered that mountain by myself, without my dad. Our hikes were more enjoyable after that.

I was nine years old when I played in a tournament in Staunton, Virginia. It was the Stuart's Draft All-Stars against the Northeast Augusta All-Stars.

We hated them. They hated us.

It was a morning game. I was playing third base and made a routine play in the first inning. But no play in Little League is routine—there is inconceivably enormous room for error on a groundball to the shortstop. We heard deafening cheers from the stands with every out. I never heard my dad yell, but I always thought I could discern his clap. He cupped his hands when he clapped, making it louder and more baritone than anyone else's. As we ran back to our dugout to get ready for our at-bat (I jogged), I looked up at my dad and I saw that smile. I don't know if Brooks Robinson's dad was proud of every routine grounder his son fielded, but, if he was anything like my dad, he would clap louder than anyone else on every slow roller down the third base line.

I never knew what my dad did in the bleachers during my games. I never asked him. I assumed that he watched me, his second son with the sweetest swing he'd ever seen. He never scowled at me or gave me pointers while I was practicing or when I was on the field. He just smiled. He always had a smile for me, like I had done something funny. I have a son now, so I know that look a little better. I smile now when I see my son pick up a Cheerio and put it in his mouth. It amazes me. I can only imagine seeing my son on a baseball field in shoes that he tied, taking sweet swings with a friend, pounding a glove he oiled.

Thinking about all those things—a son who could play baseball, oil gloves, and conquer mountains—that's probably what made him smile.

I batted fifth in the order, behind the coach's son. The pitcher was throwing bullets that day. The mound was only 45 feet away from home plate, so 50 mph looked like 90 mph. We went one-two-three in the first inning.

Northeast Augusta threatened in the second, putting runners on first and second with one out, but we got out of it. I didn't get any action.

Inside the on-deck circle, instead of watching the pitcher warm up, I looked at that short porch in right field. 160 feet? 170? Couldn't be more than 180 feet. The coach's son struck out. It was me, the pitcher throwing BBs, and 180 feet. I heard my dad clap. I did my pre-swing rituals, pretending to be Nomar Garciaparra. The pitcher got the sign, threw a laser chest high. I swung and missed. I settled in. Another laser, this time knee-high. Called strike. My dad said I had the best eye of anyone he'd ever known. It was a ball. I was down 0-2. I heard my dad's hands echo in a clap. Then nothing. He was waiting. The pitcher decided to throw that flat curve reserved for blowouts and tomfoolery. I stayed back and put a good swing on it, and even though I didn't get the head of the bat on it, the ball shot off and soared upward. I took off for first and watched the right fielder back up to the fence. That ball traveled 182 feet—tops. The bleachers erupted as the ball cleared the fence, barely. A home run. Instead of sprinting to second and sliding my awkward slide, the slide that left bruises on my thigh every time, I got to trot. My teammates mobbed me at home, smacked my helmet and slapped my heavyset ass.

I didn't look up to see my dad or his smile. The rest of the game was a blur. We won the game. As we walked off the field, I was yapping with my best friend Josh—my dad was holding my bat bag. My dad is 5'9", but he looked 7 feet tall that day. He may have been happier than I was. He always told us that he was a defensive Little Leaguer, said he made the all-star team on his glove alone—his .250 average was proof. But that day, he saw his son hit his first homer. Better than a first step, better than a first word, this was a home run. It was the first home run in our family—not even my brother, who was two years older, managed to put one over the fence.

After our post-game meeting with the coach, we started for the parking lot. I heard my dad call after me. He asked me if I wanted him to carry me on his shoulders to the car. He said he wouldn't mind. Said he would love to carry me like a champion to the top of the mountain—to his Chevy Cavalier. His shoulder wasn't hurting and he could handle the weight, it'd be no problem. He wrung his hands and wrinkled his forehead, lifting his eyebrows, as he asked me one more time to please let him carry me to the car. I told him no, I would walk with Josh and the coach's son, but thanks. Then I turned away. I didn't get to see the look on my dad's face. I'm not sure if he was hurt. I didn't think about it until years later. I wish I let him carry me on his shoulders.

I should have shared that moment with him. I don't talk to Josh anymore and I can't even remember the coach's son's name. But I remember the sound of my dad's hands clapping together. I remember him offering to carry me, heavyset as I was, two hundred yards to the parking lot. Later, my dad once saw me cry and beg to leave a baseball tournament because my coach had me riding the bench. He saw me quit baseball for good to start smoking, drinking, and doing things that teenagers do. He saw me make a mess of my life and drop out of college. I don't feel ashamed of those things. Maybe I should. But I don't. The only thing that shames me—and I tell him this—is not letting him carry me to the car.

I'll pay penance for it, I'm sure. I'm old enough to know the way the world works. My son will hit a home run and leave me carrying his glove and bag. And there I'll be, watching him walk away as I lug his gear across a gravel parking lot, proud and alone.

Q: Whose birthday is the contest issue released on?

A: Jackie Robinson, Nolan Ryan, and Ernie Banks (January 31)

"Meet the" Vignettes
Carey Bowman

Carey Bowman, the author of this essay, died of a rare cancer on Thanksgiving Day, 2016. He was 28 years old.

An aspiring writer at the end of his life, he spent his rowdy and rambunctious boyhood yearning to play professional baseball. The Big Leagues. The Show. In that sense he was like all other kids who play Little League ball, sleep with their jerseys on and dream of the game-winning hit. Carey loved baseball fervently, with gusto, the way Babe Ruth loved steak and ale. He fanatically followed Major League Baseball's most esoteric statistics; he traded baseball cards with a pawnbroker's predatory eye; he talked baseball incessantly and loudly; and he spent the summers of his youth hustling out singles on dusty ball diamonds across Virginia. Even after he came, like the rest of us, to the sad knowledge that his talent was insufficient to carry him to pro ball, he remained passionate about the game.

He grew up, went to college, joined the Air Force, served two tours in Afghanistan, married and fathered two sons. He loved abundantly and laughed with abandon, and no party really kicked off until he entered the room and flashed his wide smile. Cancer eventually wore him down physically, but it couldn't conquer his sense of humor, his generous spirit, or his zeal for baseball, especially for the team he had rooted for since he was six years old—the Chicago Cubs. As the 2016 season unfolded and the cancer slowly killed him, he fought to stay alive long enough to see the Cubs win it all. The team didn't disappoint him. He watched them triumph in a dramatic Game Seven of the World Series. Three weeks later, he slipped away.

 —Rex Bowman

P.S. Every word of Carey's essay is true, except this: he said my Little League batting average was .250. It wasn't. It was .205. He was a very generous son.

Q: How many pieces in *Twin Bill* history are the Cubs mentioned in?

A: 17

Illustration by Justine Backlund

The Mysterious Yankees Logo
By Joe Hitchcock

I went to school in the south of England in the early 2000s. It was a normal public school in the suburbs with blazers and ties, fights and mopeds, alcopops, Turkey Twizzlers, and low-level despair.

Nothing about myself or the school had any rightful connection to baseball. If you spoke about sports, you discussed Southampton FC. If you were a boy, you played rugby and soccer. If you were a girl, it was field hockey and netball. There was sometimes cricket in the summer, which at least involved a bat.

But, for reasons unknown, there was a six-month period, I want to say it was 2002, when all the toughest kids in the grade decided to wear Yankees hats. It was mostly the navy snapback version, but really it was anything with the logo they could get their hands on. Lots of counterfeit ones, some with glitter, even the white and pink colorway. They put them on in the mornings and at lunch until spotted by teachers, and again as soon as the bell rang at the end of the day.

It's tradition to tweak your school uniform for the walk home. It shows your allegiance. If you were a little dangerous, you'd wear your tie super short and flip up your blazer collar. If you were an indie sort of person, you'd reverse the tie completely and wear it skinny side out. Swapping blazer for a black hoodie was emo. Shirt tucked in, even after school hours, was a firm commitment to the difficult path. As my friends and I took our skate shoes from our backpacks, the kids that you tried not to make eye contact with covered their buzzed, frosted, or gelled heads. It was an unspoken, unanimous decision. None of us knew why they wore them or what the logo meant, but we thought it looked pretty cool.

That ornate, interlocking N and Y was definitely a mysterious thing to a nine-year-old in millennium UK. Sure, baseball was connected. But how? What, or where, is a Yankee? Manchester United plays soccer in Manchester. Chelsea in Chelsea. Yankee must be a New York borough, we decided. But, a Yankee must also be more than that because Jay-Z wears the logo. So does J.Lo and a bunch of other celebrities and we know they're not baseball players. How do the N and Y connect with all these US cultural imports we see on TV?

At the time, America was selling itself to the UK mostly through music. We're talking peak 2000s persona hip hop—*MTV Cribs*, gold grillz, getting shot seven times, cars-and-money, rags to riches. Millions of English children consuming thug-life with their Weetos. Studying our source materials, we found the answer: what else could the Yankees logo be but some form of gang sign, co-opted from its original meaning? Bloods. Crips. Yankees. That's why the tough kids at my school wore them.

In our white, suburban, still-forming brains, it all slotted together pretty nicely. It fed the idea of America as a mysterious melting pot of the kind still opposed by most parts of England. A place where white and Black people lived together, harmoniously or otherwise—which was alien. After Gavin, the only brown kid on our street, died of leukemia, 'minority' in the village meant the two Italian families. Wherever Yankees hats came from, it was a place where Black culture was as accessible as the national pastime.

I wasn't in a gang. My friends weren't tough. But that didn't stop us from wanting to join in. One summer, while scouring the street market in our local town for baseball hats, I found a knock-off Yankees bandanna. Thus was the birth of the Bandanna Gang. For around a month, we roamed the housing estate in our misinformed takes on the Durag, some sporting bandit masks, others wearing napkins, and one with a tea towel fastened behind his glasses like a shepherd in a Nativity play. I was de facto leader, as the only member wearing the actual Yankees logo, though my responsibilities mainly consisted of choosing the next street corner for us to hang around. We even took the Bandana Gang on holiday to France. My cousin, brother, and I appearing at post-9/11 customs with headwraps and our arms full of PlayStation wires and power adapters. At which point, we were thoroughly searched.

The fact that the Yankees hat remains an everyday fashion item is worth noting. What other piece of team merch is worn by so many non-fans? A Brazil soccer shirt, maybe. The All-Blacks rugby jersey. Perhaps it's only those franchises who have done enough to become synonymous with their sport.

Spike Lee contacted New Era in 1996, the year New York won their first World Series since '78, to request his famous custom red NY hat. Common opinion cites this as the moment the hat left the ballpark, the beginning of the separation between logo and team. Three years later, New Era became the MLB's official hat manufacturer, and another couple of years later, the Yankees hat was being worn by school kids in England who couldn't tell you the first thing about baseball.

Illustration by Mike Domina

The Bases Are Loaded and So Are We
By Carrie Thornbrugh

"I'm as high as a Georgia pine. I was psyched. I had a feeling of euphoria [....] I remember hitting a couple of batters, and the bases were loaded two or three times. The ball was small sometimes, the ball was large sometimes, sometimes I saw the catcher, sometimes I didn't. Sometimes, I tried to stare the hitter down and throw while I was looking at him. I chewed my gum until it turned to powder..."

— Dock Ellis on his no-no win against the San Diego Padres on June 12th, 1970.

It's nearing 7 p.m. and 94 degrees on a muggy-ass summer night in Richmond, Virginia and everyone in their right mind is keeping indoors to escape the heat. Nestled between a 147-year-old cemetery and a now-defunct elementary school is a rocky, overgrown baseball diamond and a gang of twenty or so ballplayers, decidedly not in their right mind. Most of the players who will show up tonight have arrived. A few wayward slackers might still make an appearance but it doesn't matter now that there's enough for a real ball game.

The ball has been chucked around, the first couple of beers went down pretty easy and Thin Lizzy has been cranked up to eleven by request. It's time to play ball.

"Remember your numbers this time, cuz I'm not telling you again. Ones at bat, twos in the field, move your asses, the cigarettes can be smoked in the field, you know that," chides Daddy, an informal team leader who's slight in frame but considerable in command. His voice carries over the chatter about the merits of micro-dosing, whether or not the town of Thornburg, VA is the worst place on earth, and a confirmation that Kevin Costner is a hunk of a man and it's a shame the Yankees playing on the *Field of Dreams* field probably haven't even seen the movie.

Since it's Monday, there's a catcher—on Friday he'll be replaced with a dusty bucket of tattered, battered, recycled baseballs several swings past their prime. But aren't we all?

And then we play. We really play. For the next three hours depending on how the used and abused bodies and second-hand equipment hold up—we play. The play is in the form of baseball, because in addition to their shared affinity for hard music and intoxicants, the play is why we're here—to lose ourselves in the distraction, release, and purpose that baseball provides. Tomorrow we return to the hard slog of work and responsibility, but tonight we play. The game is over when it's over. When the beers have all been drunk, the joints have been passed around and probably we've been playing with one outfielder for long enough we consider packing it up and calling it quits — fuck running that much this is baseball for Christ's sake. The nail in the coffin tonight is a heroic home run hit over the fence and into a nearby front yard, from the dugout I yell my favorite homer catchphrase that surprisingly still hasn't caught on, *"Hippies use the side doooor!"* The ball is outta here, practice is over, now we wait for the weekend game.

This is where it gets really good. The fucking game. You could also call it a party or a celebration because that's what it truly is. A baseball game in the Dock Ellis League is more like the cosmic clang that happens when play becomes abandon. All the Monday and Friday practices lead to this moment. A drug-fueled, nostalgia-tinged weekend for these punkmetalfreaks to play ball and feel like the only people to ever do so. The excitement and anticipation alone is enough to get you drunk. Taking the field on game day is like stepping into a glass of champagne—effervescent in its possibility and promise for both fun or folly.

It's important to note these players and this league while the "Sandlot Revolution" is having its moment. Although, back in 2014 when the Dock Ellis League formed, it likely would have considered itself as such—it now occupies a space outside of the current sandlot movement.

Like so many movements before it, the Sandlot Revolution has grown significantly over the last seven or so years. What started as a response to the over-organized, over-regulated, jock-centric adult intramural sports leagues have now become a mainstream, manicured, self-aware brand of baseball with high profile teams like the Texas Playboys out of Austin, TX, a team made up of professional creative types that now boast their own baseball facility, merchandise, and an impressive marketing and production team that has earned itself sponsors and collectively over 10,000 social media followers. The Playboys play other similar teams, most notably Jack White's own team bankrolled, suited, and booted by Third Man Records and equipped by Warstic.

But it's not so with the lowly Dock Ellis League. Sure, most of the teams have their own Instagram pages where they share info about practices, retro baseball memes, or shakily recorded videos of someone finally sliding safe into home or making a beautiful catch in the outfield but it's an afterthought. Really, they just came to play. I'm no exception. But I feel truly lucky to have stumbled upon these "bruised bastards of baseball" at a time in my life when I was desperately in search of a community. I had recently relocated to Richmond from San Francisco and the stars aligned and positioned my house on the very same street as the run-down practice field lovingly known as "The Scrapyard." The rest, as they say, is history. The healing salve on my lonely, uprooted life was baseball.

The Dock Ellis League is a self-proclaimed punk baseball league named in homage of our collective hero, the late great Pittsburgh Pirate, Dock Ellis who infamously pitched a no-no against the San Diego Padres in 1970 while on LSD. The league got its start in Pittsburgh, PA and spread to Philly, Virginia, and Kansas City. Mostly made up of struggling musicians, artists, bartenders, tradesmen, and other various ne'er do wells—real work hard, play hard types. Along with the palpable rough and tumble vibe the defining characteristic is the open-mindedness, respect, and egalitarian approach to the league. If you came to party, then do so. If you're a lifelong student of the game and want to play your heart out then have at it. If you've never touched a baseball in your life but are curious then give it a try. All are welcome and we mean that. The only things not tolerated are intolerance, managers, and umpires. These players govern themselves. Everyone gets to play no matter how great or shitty you are and the rules are simple:

- Don't be an asshole

- Everyone bats and you can only strikeout swinging

- No stealing

- Must be at least one female-identifying player in the field (this last rule isn't hard as the league is made up of men, women, and non-binary folks.)

Other than these exceptions—the game is played exactly as it is meant to be played. The bar for entry is non-existent, the level of play is such that if you make contact with the ball, you'll likely get on base due to the frequency of error. But this actually works in the league's favor creating fast-paced, nail biters in which a team leading by ten runs can still easily lose, verifying the famous Ted Williams quote *"Baseball is the only field of endeavor where a man can succeed three times out of ten and be considered a good performer."* This aphorism has never been more true than in the Dock Ellis League.

The traveling team piles into a convoy of beat-up vans, pickup trucks, motorcycles, and Honda Civics of the 1990s persuasion—whoever's car can handle the average six-hour drive. The home team labors together with push lawnmowers, rakes, shovels, and bent backs to groom the typically neglected public field and make it as playable as possible. Everyone chips in for hot dogs, veggie burgers, and beer and takes turns housing the visiting team in backyards, couches, and available floor space in their homes.

The game takes on a life of its own sometimes featuring live music, impromptu tattooing, post-game home run derbies, and perhaps an amateur WrestleMania match to add to the festivities. Friends, family, and bemused neighborhood onlookers join the fun, fanfare, and morbid curiosity as these out-of-shape lost boys and girls play ball.

Some teams are more organized than others and uniforms range from thrift store Hawaiian shirts to tie-dyed tees and home screen-printed raglans and jeans, shorts, sneakers, cleats or whatever really. To the untrained eye, the collection of hairy, pierced, tattooed, unkempt 35+-year-olds are indistinguishable from one another, but the teams have been playing together for so long everybody knows each other, which makes the weekend feel more like a reunion than a competition. If a team is down a few players, they'll borrow some or maybe a brave soul from the crowd will step up to the plate...literally.

To reference the dean of counterculture, George Carlin (another hero of the Dock Ellis League), it makes complete sense to us that baseball begins in the spring, the season of new life. Between April and August, the teams take turns traveling and hosting on weekends when enough people are available and the season culminates over Labor Day weekend when all the teams converge in Marlington, West Virginia for three, raucous, baseball-filled days. Over 100 people camp out at a rented campground in the mountains that are located about 20 minutes from a public baseball park with three fields and a freshwater stream flowing behind it to keep our bodies and beer cool in between games. We play for three days straight, rain or shine, hungover, strung out, or sober if you like. Each team takes turns cooking dinner and breakfast for the entire group and although everyone brings their own supplies, snacks, booze, and class A's are shared freely.

The last night, a makeshift trophy invented by the previous year's champion is presented to the new World Series Champs (the team that won the most games that weekend) and the holy ones are anointed with a bonfire fueled by the broken bats the teams have saved throughout the season—a beloved and sacred ritual offering to appease the baseball gods. Come Monday morning, with the bat embers still burning, everyone partied out and worse for the wear, pack up for the long drive home blast the only radio station in reception in the WV mountains playing the old-timey worker's rights songs of the '30s and '40s—a fitting farewell to these baseball-loving freaks who work hard and play harder. To keep the metaphors and George Carlin references going, it is no surprise then that the profound poetic beauty of baseball is epitomized in its sole objective: *to return home and to be safe.*=

Q: What team do Carrie Thornbrugh and Mike Domina play for?

A: Richmond Scrappers

Illustration by Matt Lawrence

A Career
By Francois and Nic Bereaud

February 2006: San Diego CA.

The previous June, Nic had asked for a baseball glove for his tenth birthday. Shit, I thought I'd dodged that bullet. I'd coached his youth soccer team for three years. Neither of us were much good at it, but we'd endured. I figured we each had one season left. He'd also played youth basketball – poorly – but the games were quick and fun. But baseball? I'd had a miserable time in Little League gathering one hit per season over three years. And the games were long and the parents intense. Shit. But he was an obsessive kid, I knew an idea, once planted, would stick.

The glove was black and cheap but brand name, Wilson maybe. Nic would remember. I knew enough to know that we lived in a community where Little League was important and that he'd be five years behind some kids. We played catch. I hit ground balls off his shins until it got dark. I found the closest batting cages and watched him swing until I was unwilling to spend more money on tokens.

He was assigned to the Volcanoes, Minors division, Coach Abel. There were a few weeks of practice before the first game. I tried not to watch any of it. And then there was this. For months, Nic had one question for me: "Dad, if I hit a home run in my first at-bat, will you cheer?" I assured him that I would, but I also stressed that there were many outcomes of an at-bat, of which a homer was one of the least likely. I emphasized strikeouts, ground-outs, and walks.

The big day arrived. The game was on a make-shift field behind the middle school. I showed up just before the first pitch and stood atop the small bleachers. I was impressed to see that a decent fence had been erected and the baselines were freshly chalked. The umpire was suited up and kids looked like mini-pros in their full uniforms. We had ourselves a baseball game.

The Volcanoes batted first. The lead-off hitter, a girl who appeared to be one of the team's bright spots, walked on some wild pitches. The next kid struck out on some wild pitches. Nic was up. A runner on base with one out. Dammit, a pressure situation. *What the hell am I thinking?* I shifted weight from one leg to the other.

First pitch right down the middle, bat stays on shoulder, strike one. *Oh no, the pitcher is settling in.* Settling in? He's ten. I'm already an insane parent. Second pitch, repeat of the first. Strike two. The assistant coach calls out, "Nic, you can swing." I bite my lip. *I knew this was a bad idea.* The third pitch looks exactly like the first two.

Except Nic swings. And he connects. And the ball sails. To right center or left center. I have no idea. But it sails over some kid's head and lands on the other side of the fence. Which makes it a home run. A real home run. Nic jogs around the bases. The coaches probably yell something celebratory. I can't say.

I stand stunned, body frozen. I don't cheer.

***

May 2018: Instagram post a few hours following a brutal season-ending loss for the CSULA Golden Eagles in the CCAA (Div II) Conference Tournament. Stockton CA.

It had to come to an end. All things do. I've played my last baseball game. It sucked. I shed a tear as I write this but I find comfort in knowing that nothing in my life has been as important to me as this beautiful, difficult, stupid, frustrating, and wonderful game. I owe so many people thank yous and I

81

could never cover them with due respect … but to my coaches: I thank you for your wisdom and guidance. I will be stealing everything I've learned. To my family: thank you for always supporting me … driving me to games, buying me cleats, sitting in the sun, coming to see me play because you knew I loved it … I cannot ever thank you enough. To my teammates: I owe it all to you. I'd be nothing without my team. The Volcanoes, White Sox, A's, A's, Torrey's, The Conquistadors, The Vaqueros, The Halos, and the Golden Eagles, and anyone else I've played with. You guys are family and you've given me meaning. Thank you to everyone who's ever rooted me on or wished me good luck or come to watch me play. This game means so much to me and the fact that people cheered me on to play a game, is still hard to believe. Not sure what to do next … I guess I'll figure it out. Thank you.

***

In twelve years, a boy becomes a man. A dad gets grayer. It remains a bad idea to throw behind the runner but the efficacy of bunting is debated.

Baseball is rough on the parent. It's not a team sport. There's a whole lot of nothing then, with little warning, your kid's in the spotlight. Guy on second, two outs, down a run, late innings. He's up. It's torture and, more often than not, failure. The successes amplify the pressure. You wince whenever someone shouts, "Hit a bomb." You hope the kid is oblivious.

Coaches talk incessantly. Metaphors relating the game to life are as abundant as sunflower seeds. Night games are too cold, day games too hot.

You miss it.

Q: When did Francois Bereaud become *The Twin Bill*'s fiction editor?

A: February 2024

"Meet the" Vignettes

Francois Bereaud

Who are you?

I'm a San Diego based writer and editor. I've been published widely in online and print journals, serve as the fiction editor for *The Twin Bill.*

What was the inspiration for your piece?

The inspiration for *A Career* was my son, Nic's, Instagram post from an hour or so after his college career ended with a devastating playoff loss. I was very moved by his ability to reflect on how much baseball had given him over the years, even as I knew he was so disappointed. That reflection sat with me for a few years until I had the idea to bookend it with my parent perspective on the beginning and ending of his baseball career.

What's your favorite team?

In truth, I'm not always been the best baseball fan. It took Nic's immersion in the sport and watching 100s of his games to reignite a dormant interest in the sport. As a kid I liked the A's and Joe Rudi was my favorite player. Now I root for the hometown Padres.

What's your favorite baseball memory?

My favorite baseball memory is the one I describe in the beginning of the piece, Nic's first little league at-bat.

What's the highlight of your writing career?

I recently released my first collection, *San Diego Stories*, which has been a huge highlight in my writing career.

Favorite baseball book?

I can't point to one baseball article or book as a favorite, but I can say that the writers who submit to *The Twin Bill* amaze me every publishing cycle. Each issue has some absolute gems as evidenced by this anthology.

Q: *Early Innings* was released on March 18, the birthday of which writer who created the character on the cover?

A: George Plimpton

Illustration by Sam Williams

The Home Run Jacket, or Learning How to Celebrate
By Paddy Johnston

Growing up in England in the 1990s, I went to church on Sundays, but the true religion of my people was football, or what baseball fans will most likely call soccer. Our hymns were football chants, boorish songs sung on hard concrete terraces; our gods were men in short shorts and bright shirts, with mustaches and mullets; we prayed for the gift of golden feet. Football was everywhere, and it was everything.

Football was my first experience of being in a team, and my first experience of being treated with absolute disdain by teammates. Aged about seven or eight, I'd just learned the meaning of the word 'crap,' which seems innocuous enough looking back as a man in my early thirties, but at the time felt as devastating as an f-bomb or c-bomb, with all swearing being punishable by the removal of access to the Sega Mega Drive. The first time I heard the word 'crap' in the wild was from a teammate when playing football, and not even to my face. Instead, it was whispered behind my back, just loud enough for me to hear, before being followed by cutting laughter. To be crap at football was to be crap at life, to be crap at being, to be just, well, crap. Completely crap.

Team sports were tarnished for me from that moment on, and it wasn't until decades later that I was able to admit to myself that playing in a team didn't have to be an exercise in the aggressive denigration of peers, in motivating people to succeed in a shared goal through endless stick and no carrot (carrots being, presumably, for soft wankers who can't kick). It was baseball that showed me things could be different.

I have *Peanuts* comics to thank for this, in large part. We had a lot of them lying around the house when I was a kid, and this was where the foundation of my baseball knowledge came from. Charlie Brown's struggles on the mound were something I could relate to directly, and his verbal assaults from Lucy were reminiscent of the ones I'd endured in the playground when attempting to kick the football or stop it from ending up in the goal. I fixated on them, of course, empathizing with Charlie Brown as everyone does, but I also, somewhere deep in my mind, took note of the rest of Charlie Brown's teammates. Most importantly, the pep talks he received from Schroeder as his catcher and Linus as his second baseman and statistician were more towards gentle encouragement and support, if not as overtly positive in their content as the coaching of today's *Ted Lasso*. Somewhere in my mind, the seed of baseball as a fun sport that might be for me was planted by Charles M. Schulz. It took quite a while for it to grow into a tree, however.

The other things that drew me into baseball as an English fan were the aesthetics, the history, the endless stories, and the distance it had from my own experience and that of my peers. But I also appreciated the struggle of the individual within the team, and one of the things I loved the most about watching baseball as a new fan of the game, when I started watching it out of curiosity around a decade ago, was watching teams celebrate. You don't need to know what the infield fly rule is to enjoy a team running out of the dugout to pour Gatorade over the head of the rookie who just hit his first walk-off home run, or know how many career saves a closer has when you see him hug the catcher after getting the final strikeout of the game. These are some of my favorite baseball moments, and some of the things that watered that seed, fighting off the demon of childhood sports trauma and letting the tree grow.

I started following the Blue Jays when I got into baseball because I'd had a pennant of theirs on my wall as a child. My dad worked in sports PR for a while, and he'd come by the pennant through work somehow and stuck it there in my room. I never connected it with football; it was something else entirely, and it was lost in a house move a few years later, but it also planted a seed of fandom. As a Blue Jays fan, some years later when Jose Bautista did his Bat Flip for the Ages, I watched with absolute unbridled joy as the stadium erupted. But my eyes were on his teammates and not on the fans. The channeling of such overwhelming emotion into this positivity and joy was something I knew I'd never found in football and had always wanted, but that I finally found in baseball.

Every sport has celebration, of course, but as a baseball fan it's something I've connected with on many levels, and it's helped me on the journey of self-acceptance and of acceptance of others. I pitch on a baseball team here in England now, and I love all my teammates with the joyful, celebratory love that comes with sharing team goals.

What prompted me to write this essay, however, is the 2021 Blue Jays' home run jacket.

Whenever a Blue Jay hits a home run, this blazer decorated with their logo along with all the nations their teammates come from is placed on their shoulders when they return to the dugout. Seeing the team celebrate all their home countries is a welcome sight to a baseball fan from outside the US, and a nicely performative gesture of inclusion that's served to increase my feeling of being included in sports in general as I've watched the Blue Jays this season. Baseball may be an American sport, but watching Canada's only MLB team celebrate its players' heritage in this way has shown me that baseball is for everyone, wherever you are in the world.

The joy on the Blue Jays' faces when wearing the jacket, or bestowing it on a teammate, is boyish and pure, and it's been my favorite thing this season. You're always on a journey as a baseball fan, but the home run jacket has shown me how far I've come, as all I see now in sport is joy, celebration, and the uplifting of teammates, and I have baseball to thank for that.

Q: Which country did *The Twin Bill*'s four founding editors meet in?

A: England

"Meet the" Vignettes

Paddy Johnston

Who are you?

I'm Paddy Johnston from Surrey, England. By day I work in Communications for a news agency. I write fiction and non-fiction as much as I can when I'm not working or chasing my two young sons around, or producing music and podcasts.

What was the inspiration for your piece?

My piece is about the 2021 Blue Jays and their home run jacket, which was decorated with the home countries of all their players. I wanted to share some of my thoughts on how this exemplified inclusion in sport, in contrast to my own experiences growing up in England, where I felt excluded from sport. Baseball was the sport that finally clicked for me after decades of thinking sport wasn't for me, so I always enjoy writing about things that exemplify this, like home run celebrations.

What's your favorite team?

The Blue Jays! I chose them because of a pennant that somehow ended up on my childhood bedroom wall. I love that they're the only Canadian team in MLB, and they have a fascinating history as well as one of the best logos and overall aesthetics among MLB teams (in my opinion).

Who is your favorite player?

Can I have two? I usually choose R.A. Dickey, who was a great pitcher during the Blue Jays' 2015 and 2016 seasons, which I got a little too invested in as they made their playoff pushes. He was a true underdog: knuckleballer late in his career who had bounced around a few teams and had a rocky road to the majors. I always enjoyed his dad vibes.

My other favourite is Curtis Granderson, who played one season for the Jays late in his career and didn't throw up any amazing stats, but was by all accounts a legendary dude and the exemplary 'clubhouse guy' who everyone seemed to love. He always played with 'don't think, have fun' written inside his hat, and I've tried to live by those words ever since I read about that. I have them written inside my own team hat. I'll also give an honourable mention to Jose Bautista, who is covered in the next question.

What's your favorite baseball memory?

Probably Jose Bautista's bat flip. I wasn't watching live as the time was unsociable for the UK, but I remember opening my phone and seeing the clips and watching the highlights and feeling the surge of collective joy that one of the best players in my team had done something amazing: celebratory, epic, just a little obnoxious, a power move, a delight to all Jays fans.

A different one would be my first time pitching in a game. I play in UK single-A, so it's not like it's that tough, but I was terrified and elated all at once. I managed to get a strikeout on a splitter, which was the greatest feeling, even if I did go on to allow three earned runs after that!

What's the highlight of your writing career?

Putting out my book, *Stealing Home: Rookie Season*, which is a collection of essays from an email newsletter I used to do regularly about baseball, with illustrations by *Twin Bill* legend and fellow British baseball fan Sam Williams. Working on those together was always really fulfilling and connected us a lot as friends and fans, and the book was a culmination of the fun we had putting those together.

What's your favorite baseball book?

My favourite book on baseball is *Baseball Life Advice* by Stacey May Fowles. She's a Jays fan like me and articulates the highs and lows of fandom and how we connect it to our own experiences in the most incredible, passionate, open way. Reading that book helped me to formulate my love of baseball and to understand why I connected with it when no other sport had given me the same thing. I'd recommend it to any baseball fan.

Cardboard Heroes by Gary Hoff

Collector's Item
By Linda Petrucelli

The dial-up modem dings and the AOL metallic voice buzzes, You've got mail! You type in the CNBC address and fill out the form. *The Suze Orman Show*, not-to-be-missed Saturday night TV with Susan Lynn "Suze" Orman, guru to the fabulous but broke. The Tips for Prospective Guests advise, no run-of-the-mill financial question will do. The important thing is that there's conflict so the audience can take sides.

The Trans-Pacific moving man, straining in his coveralls, swaddled the trunk with sheeting like Saran Wrap, and sealed the wooden chest into a spongy cocoon. It was the last piece of furniture to be removed from our East Village apartment.

"Take good care of this." My husband laid his hand on top and let it linger. The trunk contained the bulk of his treasured baseball card collection.

"Time to say goodbye, Gary." I was sitting on the floor in the front room.

The mover tipped the chest vertical on a dolly and wheeled it out the door. Gary leaned against the threshold and watched.

"Those aren't just baseball cards," he informed the disappearing moving man. He turned toward me. "They're my childhood." I put the sheaf of papers with the estimate back into its envelope. Insurance for the baseball cards was about three times what I expected.

The night before we left on the nonstop Newark to Honolulu flight, Gary loaded his carry-ons with his most valuable cards—keepers he'd saved since a boy and collected over the last thirty years. Each precious piece of cardboard lay nestled inside acetate sheets and organized into three-ring binders. His Jackie Robinson 1948 Leaf rookie card, he would wear hidden in the inner recesses of his belly bag.

While you wait in the phone queue, the show is in progress. The producer who greenlighted your question says, Relax. We're live-to-tape. Bloopers can be edited out. You're up next. Suze has become your money mentor since you moved and changed jobs, your income cut in half. In the background, a caller wants to co-sign a car loan for her twenty-something son. Suze interrupts, You've got to be kidding me! A bar of tinny muzak blares then fades.

And it's Linda from Hawaii. Aloooooha! Or maybe I should say, Batter up?

I proposed to him on a snow-bound night in bed, with my eyes closed. We spooned and his fingers traced snowflakes on my shoulder. I didn't want to become his wife but I'd very much like to be his partner forever. He was slow to understand that I had just asked him to marry me. The next night I made ratatouille and afterward, sitting on the sofa, he took my hand, kissed my lemon garlic fingers.

"1968 Topps, Red Sox," he whispered and placed in my upturned palm, a baseball card. A fuzzy black and white photo caught a player in a body-twisting follow-through, bat flung wild over his left shoulder.

I read aloud: "Petrocelli Socks Two Homers."

"I'll never ask you to change your name."

***

"Suze, I wonder if you could umpire a fight I keep having with my husband. It's about his baseball card collection."

Girlfriend, Suze pauses for dramatic effect. Do you mind my asking about how much it's worth?

On top of the round oak table we had moved from New York to Hawaii, Gary laid out his baseball cards in a crazy quilt. He picked up a gaudy rectangle, brought it close for inspection then stretched his arm back for another view. "Warren Spahn!" Then he set the card on a tiny tripod, took out a Pentel pen, and began drawing. I was worrying through the mail on the other side of the table, but also watching him sketch.

He picked up another marker. "I learned how to draw the human form from baseball cards." His pen soared across the page, a line drive.

You grip the telephone and can't stop the fear from scattering into the receiver. "It's crazy expensive here. We'll never afford a house."

On the sketchbook page, a lanky-legged pitcher takes shape, winding up to throw a fastball. "There were no Black people where I grew up in LaCrosse. Baseball cards were my first experience with integration. They are my history."

"He won't listen to reason, Suze. I want him to keep a few and sell the rest. Use the money for a down payment or maybe invest in a Roth. Don't you think that's the financially responsible thing to do?"

"Thank God my mother never threw them away!"

Girlfriend, you make sense, financially speaking, but you know what I always say: people first…

Gary walked into the study where I had been talking on the phone.

"The producer says she'll email me the date when it's scheduled to air."

"So did she say to sell them?"

A lilikoi vine with new fruit breathed a sweetness through the jalousie windows.

"I'll never ask you to change," and a green abundance filled the room.

Q: Who won *The Twin Bill*'s 2023 Best Baseball Nonfiction Book?

A: Adam Lazarus, *The Wingmen*

"Meet the" Vignettes

Linda Petrucelli

Who are you?
My home is on Old Camp 17 Road, a tin-roof rancher overlooking the ʻAlenuihāhā Channel, a fierce stretch of Pacific Ocean that separates the Big Island where I live from Maui. I've just planted a Royal Poinciana Tree in my back yard where one day it will grow a flaming canopy next to my Sago Palm and Plumeria Trees. I like to sit on my lanai and write most days. I'm joined by my husband Gary, Bonnie my rescue coonhound, and currently, four feral cats.

What was the inspiration for your piece?
I wrote this essay as a Valentine's Day gift for my husband. He sometimes feels awkward when I write about him and we actually had a little tiff when I told him I was going to write about his baseball card collection. When I read him the finished piece, though, he almost cried he was so happy. Talking to the financial guru herself, Suze Orman, also inspired the piece. I totally learned that money isn't everything.

What's your favorite team?
The barnstorming House of David amateur team in the '20s and '30s! They wore their hair crazy long. They allowed Babe Didrikson to pitch. They regularly played both Negro Leagues teams as well as barnstorming Major League players. Plus—they would serenade the fans with their ukulele band during the seventh inning stretch.

Who is your favorite player?
Rico Petrocelli, Red Sox infielder. I'm sure that somewhere in the Roman gene pool, we are distantly related. My husband courted me with his 1968 Topps baseball card, the one that looks like a black-and-white TV set: Petrocelli Socks Two Homers.

What's your favorite baseball memory?
Getting to hear stories from Negro League pitcher Don Troy, who my husband and I got to know in Hilo, Hawaii. Don played for the Baltimore Elite Giants in the mid 1940s and was Roy Campanella's roommate. It was towards the end of his life and he struggled with Parkinson's Disease. But when he spoke in front of my husband's elementary students, Don reverse-aged before our very eyes, telling his stories without a note, and gracefully demonstrated his pickoff move to first.

What's the highlight of your writing career?
It's a hope that always hides in the piece I'm writing at the time.

Favorite baseball book/article/movie/writer etc.
I'm from Iowa, so it's personal for me—*Shoeless Joe* by W. P. Kinsella

Illustration by Elliot Lin

Just Another Late Inning Go-Ahead Run
By Paul Ruta

Any Toronto Blue Jays fan will tell you about Joe Carter's walk-off homer that clinched the 1993 World Series. They'll tell you about José Bautista's bat flip in Texas—it's the GIF that keeps on giving. But the plays that really stick in the imagination of a true fan tend not to be the most historic or iconic.

For me, one of those is a spectacular play at the plate in a relatively meaningless interleague game by a player whose portrait will never hang in Cooperstown. My son and I watched it on a motel TV in Thunder Bay, Ontario, eating fried chicken on our beds while a storm outside shrink-wrapped our rented SUV in a quarter-inch of ice.

In spring 2017 my son had graduated from the University of British Columbia and the two of us were on a weeklong road trip back to Toronto in a Mazda filled with the usual college guy stuff: plastic bags of insufficiently laundered clothes, hockey equipment that has never been laundered, a hookah and a couple of books. April weather in Vancouver was typically balmy and the flowers and leaves were out. It stayed mostly sunny and dry for the four-day drive through the Rockies and across the Prairies as well. Smooth sailing, meteorologically speaking.

The minute we crossed the Manitoba border into Ontario, though, we entered some kind of alternative Twilight Zone reality where, no matter what time of year it is, it's always a crappy day in February. It was freezing. There was snow. We assumed, as naive Torontonians, that this weather must be joking and would soon give it up. We stopped for lunch in the town of Kenora and learned that the weather wasn't joking. In fact, we heard rumors of worse weather on the way—rumors that turned out to be all too true.

By the time we reached Thunder Bay, on the western edge of Lake Superior, rain was pelting in sideways and froze as it landed, coating everything, turning the entire city into a museum of glass. We were lucky to find a comfortable motel with a KFC around the corner. We made it back to the room with a bucket in time for the game.

The Blue Jays were playing the Cardinals in St. Louis. It was an uneventful game, heading into the seventh inning tied at two. There hadn't been much action for commentators Buck Martinez and Pat Tabler to discuss except to mention the arrival of outfielder Chris Coghlan, who had signed with the Jays two weeks before. Coghlan had been National League Rookie of the Year in 2009 with the Marlins, then found himself with the Cubs when they won the 2016 World Series. Otherwise he was an unremarkable player with a career .258 batting average.

Unremarkable, that is, until the top of the seventh inning.

Coghlan reached on a walk before Kevin Pillar ripped a double (later scored a triple) off the right field wall. When St. Louis outfielder Stephen Piscotty misplayed the ball, the Jays saw their chance to score and waved home the runner.

Piscotty's throw was weak and bounced several times, forcing catcher Yadier Molina to move away from the plate by a couple of steps towards third base.

By this time the sprinting Coghlan had rounded third base and was heading for a sure collision with Molina—and a sure out—when the most remarkable, most hitherto un-Coghlan-like thing happened: he went airborne. Vaulting clean over the crouching Molina in an acrobatic head-first dive, he touched the vacated home plate squarely with one hand, scoring the go-ahead run, rolled into a forward somersault, sprang to his feet in one smooth movement and trotted nonchalantly to the dugout.

The crowd in the stands went nuts.

From our motel room we could almost hear television sets across Canada exploding with excitement.

Yadier Molina never knew what didn't hit him.

Bucky and Pat said that they'd never seen a run-scoring play quite like that before—and those guys have seen everything in baseball.

The Blue Jays went on to win in extra innings, not that anybody remembers that detail about the game. The sad coda to his highlight-reel performance is that Chris Coghlan was released by the Jays that August, after less than five months with the team, effectively ending his major league career.

In the morning, it took half an hour to chip off enough ice with a credit card to open the Mazda's door. (Three guesses where the snow brush was.) That day we snaked along the slippery Trans-Canada Highway as far as Marathon, a gold-mining village not quite halfway around the top of Lake Superior. At midday we learned that the provincial police planned to close the highway because of unsafe driving conditions. We had no choice but to spend the night in Marathon.

Things seemed to have cleared up by morning and the roads reopened. However, once we were gassed up and back on the highway with a pair of large coffees and a box of donuts, the weather turned again. What we had hoped would be a scenic drive along the north shore of Lake Superior turned into a daylong white-knuckle express on the winding Trans-Canada Highway, following the taillights of 18-wheelers in near-whiteout conditions. We never so much as caught a glimpse of the lake the whole way to Sault Ste. Marie.

My son and I still reminisce about that trip. The majesty of Banff and Lake Louise; the modern architecture of Calgary; the wide-open Prairies and the sunshine and warmth of Winnipeg—and how we somehow navigated that improbable Northern Ontario ice storm without landing in a ditch.

And, of course, we'll never forget Chris Coghlan's giant leap into the hearts and minds of baseball fans across the country.

Q: Which country does founding CNF editor Joe Hitchcock live in?

A: Canada

"Meet the" Vignettes
Paul Ruta

Who are you?
I was born and raised in Niagara Falls, Ontario. That's me in the background of your holiday snapshots. I'm a writer by trade and have survived a long advertising career in Toronto, Singapore and Hong Kong. Married with 3 adult children, all of us living in London now. Interests are cats, grilled cheese, WWII documentaries, guitars and manual transmissions.

What's your favorite team?
I have two favorite teams: Toronto Blue Jays and whoever's playing the Yankees.

Who is your favorite player?
Ichiro Suzuki, duh. Being Canadian, I must also salute Ferguson Jenkins, Larry Walker, Justin Morneau, Jordan Romano, Paul Quantrill, Russell Martin, Freddie Freeman, Eric Gagné, Joey Votto, Jason Bay and Vladimir Guerrero Jr among dozens more major leaguers who make our country proud, including the man with the greatest baseball name in the history of the sport, Stubby Clapp.

What's your favorite baseball memory?
I get a little thrill whenever I visit a ballpark for the first time. Faves are PNC Park, Petco Park, Dodger Stadium, Oracle Park, Comerica Park and the Green Monster at Fenway. Also AAA Durham and Buffalo's Pilot Field (or whatever they've changed the name to lately).

What's the highlight of your writing career?
I wrote a middle-grade chapter book under the pen name Andy Spearman. It sold okay but more rewarding is that for many years it appeared on summer reading lists of recommended humor books for kids by schools, libraries and nerdy independent list-makers all over North America.

Favorite baseball book?
W.P. Kinsella is a Canadian who wrote a great deal about baseball, most famously his fine first novel, *Shoeless Joe,* which was adapted into the fine movie, *Field of Dreams.*

Q: How many countries have *The Twin Bill* contributors been from?
A: 6. United States, Canada, England, Spain, Australia, Belgium.

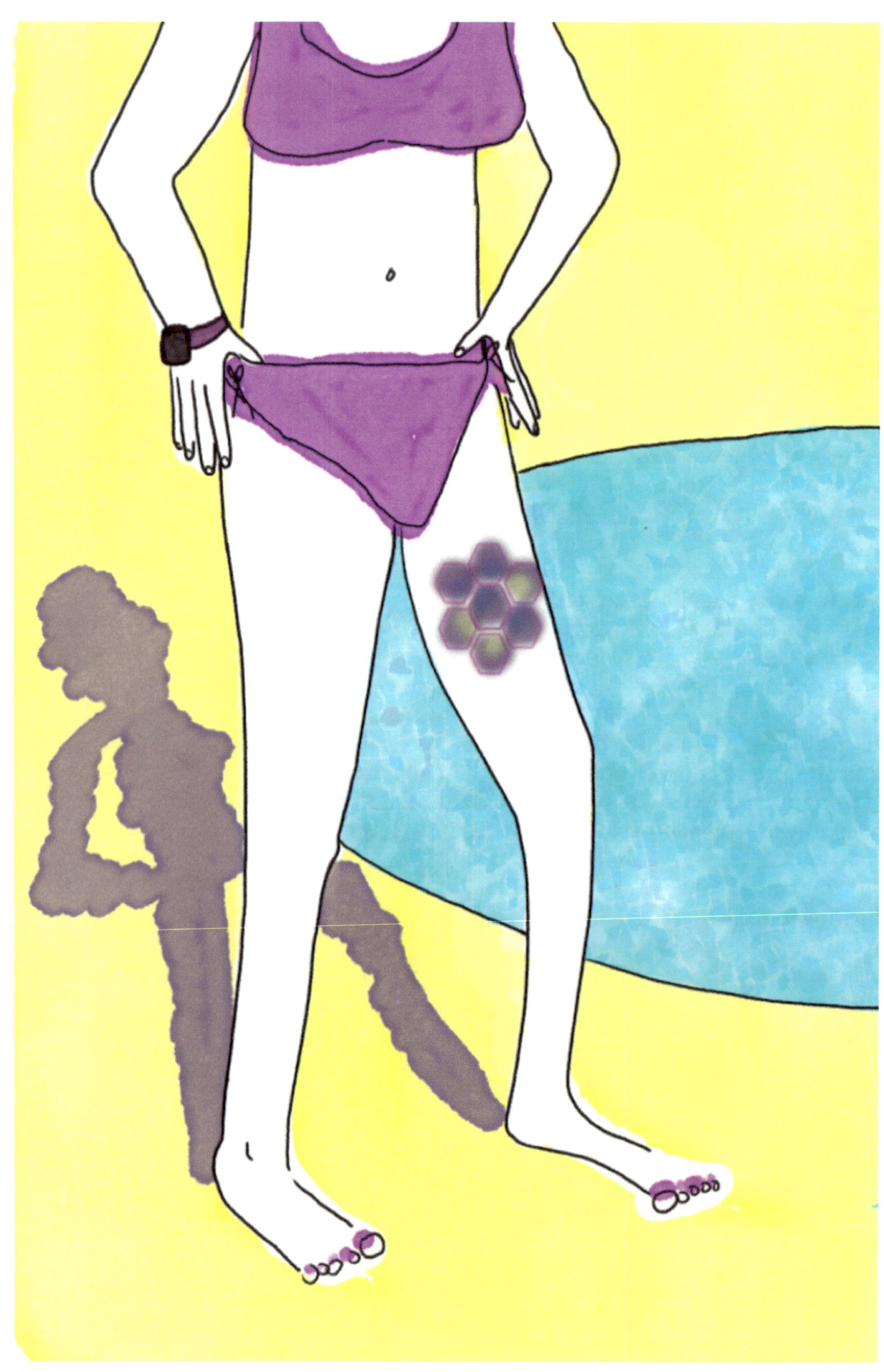

Illustration by Caite McNeil

Ball Mark
By Ruth Hawley

I remember when Mom showed me her permanent one. It was made of spidery purple pentagons on her upper, inner thigh. I remember the shock of pain that seared my own skin, the first time that I got one, and how I grew to love the hurt. Wondering if this would be the one that stuck with me for good.

If nothing else, it would be the trophy I paraded around the swimming pool in my bikini. A ball mark was my way of showing the world that I was tough.

Now that I've hung up my cleats, I wonder what scabs I have to show that I am fabulous. Scabulous is a real word, you know. It's the pride one has for a scar on her body.

So what do I have now? Without my ball mark?

Perhaps the pawprint from my puppy, turned green and yellow since the days she jumped on my legs in greeting.

"Olive, no! Bad!" I yelled as hard as I could at her so she could learn.

But part of me hopes she never does. There's something about a too-well-trained dog that makes me sad. At least that's what I tell my bruises on my soft inner thighs at night, before we go to bed.

Q: How many CNF pieces has *The Twin Bill* published in their first 16 issues?

A: 68

Illustration by Elliot Lin

On Disappearing
By Malavika Praseed

In 2021, pitcher Kumar Rocker does not sign with the New York Mets, who have drafted him in the first round of the MLB draft. Instead, he signs the next year with the Texas Rangers, seven spots higher. His father is Tracy Rocker, an African-American former NFL lineman. His mother's parents are from India. In baseball, African Americans are disappearing. In all sports on this soil, Indians exist in a constant state of disappearing, if they have ever once arrived.

Kumar Rocker at Vanderbilt University: 2.89 ERA, 28-10 record, 2 complete games.

My academic resume in hopes of the Vanderbilt University biology program: 4.75 GPA, 34 ACT, a smattering of extracurriculars, application denied.

Cricket exists as a parallel state. My father plays games with his classmates after school and on Sundays. Saibaba Colony, Coimbatore is one of the largest districts in the city, and by all metrics, it boasts many parks. But I see these games on dirt. Clouds of dust kicked up as the stitched cork ball hits dirt and spins, whirls, past the batsman through the wickets. Or makes contact against the broad wood bat and sails over fences. "If you threw like in baseball," my father tells me, "everyone would crush them." I imagine baseball players wielding cricket bats like caveman clubs behind their backs.

Along with the pitches, my father scoffs at gloves. In cricket, you catch barehanded. You may break fingers, the game goes on. He scoffs, especially, at spectators with gloves in the stand. 2010, we stand past the right field foul pole at Tropicana Field. He reaches out and snags an arcing foul ball. The crowd roars and screams. I clamor for the little white jewel in his hand, which he offers to a five-year-old on his left. I am fifteen and too old to cry for justice.

Two of the sports my father learns to love in Tampa are sports that should not exist in Tampa. Because it rains nearly daily in the summer, they build an ugly tin dome in the shape of a sliced orange and play baseball on artificial grass. Because it is warm in Tampa, they create an indoor freezer and the ice skates come out for hockey. Basketball, he says, was once beautiful. He immigrated to America in the early 1990s, Chicago, Illinois. His first impression was peak MJ soaring through the sky.

Football is the least intuitive sport. To teach it to me, my father draws the field on a yellow piece of paper. Thin black lines, broad sketches. Years before, his father teaches me how to draw with those same black lines. Years before, his father-in-law makes me practice writing with those same black lines. Years after all of this, my father will try to recreate football again for my sister. It doesn't take, though she does learn to draw, and I learn to write.

In 2021, I interview sportswriter Jeff Pearlman for my fledgling podcast with fifty-five listeners on a good week. Jeff is incredibly kind, and there's a catch in his voice, almost disbelief, when I tell him I am twenty-five. I am twenty-five and have read Ball Four and The Natural and understand the significance of bird dogs in Pat Jordan's *A False Spring*. These are references outside my context, in youth and in skin. They are not written for me. Jeff is only a little younger than my father, and has the career I aspired to had I not been afraid. His first claim to fame was the 1998 *Sports Illustrated* expose of the bigoted former pitcher John Rocker. No relation to Kumar.

Sportswriter Kavitha Davidson has a tattoo of the New York Yankees logo. She co-wrote the book *Loving Sports When They Don't Love You Back*. For this book I forgive her heretical fandom. People pronounce her name Kah-VEE-tha, rather than the first-syllable emphasis KAV-ih-tha. Translated from the Sanskrit, her name means poetry. We all make these concessions.

It is not Kavitha or Jeff I idolize as a child, but Hannah Storm. She stands in front of the screen in her smart dresses and lays out the game in front of us. I watch her every morning with a bowl of cereal between my knees as I wait for the bus. She has a deep voice and short hair and is not classically, blondly beautiful. This signals that we are to take her seriously. I imagine she writes all her own coverage and tears through stadiums for the story, even though this is not true. I google *Hannah Storm clothes* and look like a corporate lawyer in my ninth grade classrooms. Smart pencil skirts above knobby, hairy legs. I walk across classrooms in my heels, and boys in their seats clomp-clomp their feet to the time of my steps. I retreat into t-shirts. My short hair and deep voice mean nothing.

Total population of India: 1.408 billion

Total Olympic medals won: 35

Total golds: 10

My only athletic feat is memorization, better suited to spelling bees. Beyond my father and I playing catch in our backyard, I wilt and crumble when faced with a ball. The first time I faint is on the tennis court. The second time, at fifth grade softball tryouts where I am the only one not to make the team. I will faint several more times between then and now, the worst of which occurs on an underground train in Barcelona, where I am coaxed awake by a donut shop employee with a cup of sugar water. There was no ball then. No real excuse.

Total population of India: 1.408 billion

Males in excess: 54.2 million

My father claims he has never wanted sons. He wanted two daughters and received them, my sister and me. But eventually someone takes my place in bat and ball games. My father swings wildly, launches the yellow softball against purple metal bat, and his companion runs to retrieve. Butter leaps across the grass, grabs and fetches, then he rears up for the next swing. All four yellow legs bound off the ground. Butter's successor, Biscuit, is more of a soccer player, a wrestler, an overall ne'er-do-well. My father wants for nothing, not even sons.

In 2008, right fielder Rocco Baldelli cannot recover from injury, cannot run the bases, cannot perform at the standard set by his position and salary. He peters out of the lineup, sees specialist after specialist, is made a free agent by the Tampa Bay Rays, and is later diagnosed with a rare mitochondrial channelopathy. In 2008, a thirteen-year-old girl develops a nascent interest in medicine. She will write her undergraduate thesis on the care and treatment of mitochondrial disease, and present her paper with Rocco's face attached. She will cite him whenever asked in all her interviews for genetic counseling school, and she will think about him as she guides patients through the uncharted waters of unknown diagnoses. She will wonder if he faints.

His disappearance from athletics will lead, indirectly, to the appearance of an Indian elsewhere.

Total number of active Major League Baseball players: 975

Total number of certified genetic counselors: 5,629

The hardest session of my career concerns a young Indian couple seeking elective twin reduction in the first trimester. Their reasons are unspoken, their reasons are not my business. They ask few questions during the bulk of the session, only to ask, more than once, if it is true that both fetuses are girls. Can we be sure? The session is hard because I am young, inexperienced, and cannot compartmentalize myself. Our professional creed is nondirectiveness. I summon almost none for this couple. My voice is flat, matter-of-fact, my vowels clipped. I wonder if the two of them stem from some princedom where only male heirs can inherit the land. Or if it's sports. Either way, this father wants sons. *Get a dog,* I want to say. *Or teach your girls to play.*

In 2023, the Toronto Blue Jays select third baseman Arjun Nimmala in the first round of the MLB Draft. He is seventeen years old and boasts Indian heritage on both sides. Like my father, he grew up playing cricket. Like my father, he is full of hope. His name means archer, warrior, harking back to the mythical Arjuna of *Mahabharata* fame. Hero of heroes. His name is one my husband and I have considered, in the future, for a boy.

Baseball stadiums I have seen with my father: 4 (Tampa, Chicago, Chicago, Cleveland).

Baseball stadiums I have seen with my husband: 8 (Tampa, Chicago, Chicago, Cleveland, St. Louis, Milwaukee, New York, New York).

In 2023, Kumar Rocker leaves single-A ball in need of Tommy John surgery, ending his season, possibly ending his career. The repair of the UCL remains the most tenuous procedure in all of baseball. It is unknown if, even with this surgery, if he will rise to visibility. As fast as we appear, we disappear.

"Meet the" Vignettes
Malavika Praseed

Basically, who are you? Where do you live, what do you do, etc.

I'm Malavika Praseed, I live in the Chicago area with my husband, daughter, and cat. I'm a cancer genetic counselor by trade and a writer by passion, and am currently working on my first novel.

What was the inspiration for your piece?

In my MFA curriculum we studied the braided essay, and I admired how this form allows the author to explore several related topics in one cohesive form. Drawing upon things I often think about: baseball, my identity as an Indian-American woman, my family relationships, I was able to craft this essay by exploring how these thoughts could connect.

What's your favorite team?

Even though I live in the Chicago area, I consider Tampa, FL to be my hometown and have been a lifelong fan of the Tampa Bay Rays.

Who is your favorite player?

My favorite player has always been Rocco Baldelli, former Rays outfielder and current manager of the Minnesota Twins. Beyond pure baseball ability and childhood nostalgia, Baldelli's mysterious metabolic illness that led to his premature retirement inspired my eventual career in genetics.

What's your favorite baseball memory?

Hands-down, game 162 of the 2011 season. I watched the entirety of the game live and witnessed the Rays come from behind against the Yankees and slide into the playoffs at the eleventh hour. I'll never forget it.

What's the highlight of your writing career?

2024 proved to be an exciting year in writing for me. I finished my MFA in fiction from Randolph College, found a literary agent, and started publishing my work in journals like *The Twin Bill*.

Favorite baseball writer? Book? Movie?

My favorite sportswriter is Jeff Pearlman, who has written some truly insightful longform pieces on baseball. I'm also especially drawn to Bernard Malamud's *The Natural*, which inspired me to incorporate sports and speculative elements in my own fiction. Baseball movies? Can't go wrong with *A League of Their Own*.

Q: When did Malavika Praseed become *The Twin Bill*'s CNF editor?

A: February 2024

Illustration by Travis D. Roberson

Stadium Rats
By Travis D. Roberson

Rats complain of three-day headaches as if uncertain of the cause. Certainly not the lack of sleep, the 12-hour days. Rats don't get home 'til two in the morning and when they slide their phones from their pockets and check the clock it's 8:30 AM and they're already back, prowling the tunnel beyond the employee entrance.

Rats : stadium rats : baseball season.

Rats stuff their aching feet into worn-out dress shoes (all black per uniform guidelines). To speak of sore heels and aggravated bunions is to elicit a challenge. "Oh you think your feet hurt? I did 22,000 steps yesterday." This is the only place where some might consider 22,000 steps low. These fiery twinges and searing cramps, they are marks of pride—skin-deep totems of a relentless working spirit.

A lot of rats, they couldn't care less about the crack of the bat or pop of a glove. This is about a paycheck, making rent on time, having enough in the bank account to cover your daughter's orthodontist visits. Ask any rat where their allegiances lie in the 9th inning when it's tied 0-0. That's when they abandon any and all loyalties, devotees of whichever team will send them home for a short night's rest.

Rats work the homestands. Some homestands fly by—five quick days over before a blink. But then there's the 11-game stretches with no end in sight.

Here's what rats dread:

– Tie games
– Extra innings
– Double headers
– The lingering eyes of upper management

Called rats because that's how management sees them. Rats are many and rats are expendable. Easily ~~exterminated~~ fired, easily replaced. Rats wear name tags above their right breast but overlords pay no mind to these little marks of identity, the same way they ignore rodents scurrying across subway tracks on their way home. But that's the way rats like it. The privilege of invisibility.

Rats start early, five hours before first pitch. By the 6th or 7th inning, you'll see it—the fatigue they try to squash down so they can power through the day. When the 9th inning arrives and the stadium roars with triumph or upheaval, that's when rats come alive again. Rats hear the same awful song that plays every time the home team wins and spring into action. The hungry and broke gather whatever food's left behind, nibbling on it as it's carted back to the kitchen. *"Here's some fries nobody ate. You want?"*

Rats scurry from the stadium, duties complete. Summer air slaps them when they step outside, drawing more sweat than their bodies are willing to sacrifice. It's a long walk to the trains that carry them home, the last thing their whimpering rat feet need. The air is redolent with marijuana and cigarettes. The perfume of jubilation, of making it through another day. A long homestand like this, rats take any moment they can to celebrate. Six more days, then a seven-day break. An eternity from now.

Empty seats on the train feel like a reward from God. Rats collapse into the hard plastic, prop their heads against the windows behind them. Eight stops and they'll be home. Nine stops. Two trains and then a bus.

One rat to the other: "You working tomorrow?"

Rats try to answer but all they manage is a nod. This is sufficient; the other rat nods in return.

What will the rats do when October arrives and the season ends?

There's talk of playoffs this year. The home team's doing well, sitting in first place with a sizable lead. Then again, there was talk of playoffs last year but the team blew it in the final months. Rats take it as it comes. The prospect of a postseason is a bittersweet thing. As much as rats need the work, they're also sick of it. Sick of privileged customers with their self-imposed authority. Sick of management breathing down their necks. But a longer season means more money, so they shouldn't complain…right?

Illustration by Sam Williams

The Errors of Memory
By Michael Ward

For a brief moment in my life, I was a child actor. I was eleven, and I had no interest in acting—didn't know the first thing about it—but I had a mother who did. That's how one Saturday in the early 1990s I joined hundreds of kids in a suburban Dallas high school auditorium to audition for a role in what would become one of the most popular baseball movies of that decade. It was my first audition. It was also my last. That is, if how I remember it is how it really happened.

I, like many American boys born before soccer gained any sort of popularity, began my sports career with T-ball. From there, I progressed through several years of the *whump* and eerie consistency of pitching machines. These were hours spent on tawny dirt with my dad and volunteer dad/coaches, fielding scuffed balls with ill-fitting gloves. Collecting baseball cards and searching through the Beckett to discern their value made up weekend afternoons. It was a time when movies like *The Natural* and *Field of Dreams* had imbued the sport with a new sense of fantasy and mythology. But what I did not know or understand then but know and understand now is that my heart was never in the game.

At about the same time, my mother was searching for something she could put her heart into. Like many other women of her generation, she worked until she had kids and then became a stay-at-home mom. Then when I started sixth grade and began to learn ratios and long division, she went to community college to finish her bachelor's degree. Warm light would spill onto the kitchen table in the evenings after she had taken me home from baseball practice. And there she was with thick books of college algebra and statistics. Higher education was never designed to fit a parent's lifestyle, and unfortunately, my mother never finished her degree.

She leaned toward extraversion and soon was getting work as an extra on shows like *Walker, Texas Ranger*. One day, Chuck Norris, the famed action star and eponymous "Walker," ambled onto the set. My mother's eyes grew wide at being so close to fame. When the day-long shoot was over, she returned home with memories and the buzzing excitement that comes with an imminent appearance on broadcast television.

At some point, my mother's agent informed her that a baseball movie was in production with several roles for adolescent boys. I, of course, played baseball; and I, of course, was an adolescent boy. Even though I had no inclination toward acting, I was roped into thinking that this was a role for me. I put on my little league uniform: Yankee pinstripes with our team's local business sponsor "Birdsong Electric" splashed across the back. Now was my opportunity; Hollywood was calling.

Auditions for the unnamed film were held at a local high school. Thin echoes of murmurs reverberated off the Formica floors and locker-lined walls. The casting call had brought in kids well into their teenage years. Would-be child stars towered over me, my head just reaching the top of their crisp white baseball leggings. I had never been inside a high school, much less to an audition. I was called into an auditorium with a group large enough to fill half of the front row. There, the casting producer handed out part of a script and asked us to take turns reading the lines.

The script looked as familiar to me as my mother's algebra textbook. My throat clenched.

My breathing quickened. I held the pages in my trembling hands and began to mutter, misread, and mangle the lines so badly that the crew must've thought I was in the wrong room. I knew immediately, without a glance at the disappointed faces of the casting team, that I was not getting the role. I put the script down and hung my head as I slunk back out into the hallway with all the other future child stars. In that corridor hung the stench of embarrassment and fright. So painful was the experience that I bawled from the auditorium door to the parking lot, bathed in the same abominable sunlight that engulfs you as you step out of a movie theater at midday. My mother did her best to comfort me, and I still remember the lines I tried to read.

All this came up at a dinner with my wife and my parents some months ago. My wife had known this story for a while, but I had never spoken about it with my mother in thirty years. As I retold it, my mother squinted her green eyes and cocked her head slightly. When I finished the part where we walked to the car while I was crying, my mother simply said, "I don't remember that."

"You don't remember me crying?"

"I don't recall taking you to any audition," she said.

A formative experience remembered by only one of the two people who were there felt like a betrayal. This was an event that, in my mind, we shared. What we remember and how we remember it is personal. An actor remembers her lines because she's paid to. I remember my lines because of a mild form of childhood trauma. But to learn my mother had no memory of any of this happening was tragic. An insidious notion, then, crept into my mind: did it really happen at all?

There is at least some evidence in my favor. About a year or so after my audition, I was sitting in a movie theater. There, with technicolor celluloid flashing at twenty-four frames per second, I heard the words that I had read, the words that had caused me so much distress. The movie existed and the lines were performed, thankfully, by a much better actor.

```
                        HAM

        You're killin' me, Smalls.  Look, these

        are s'mores stuff.  Pay attention:

        First, you take the graham - you put

        the chocolate on the graham.  You hold

        the chocolate on the graham while you

        roast the 'mallow.


        (He does.  The mallow flames to life.)

                    HAM (CONT'D)

        Then when the mallow's flamin', ya

        stuff it on the chocolate and cover it

        with the other end.

                        (BEAT)

        Then, you scarf.
```


In the dark, my heart skipped. Not only had I unknowingly auditioned for *The Sandlot*, which turned thirty this year, but I had also been up for the role of what Hollywood called at the time "the chubby kid" when I was the skinniest kid in school. Patrick Renna, who won the hearts of the casting team over all those thousands of other boys around the country like me, portrayed Ham.

As it happens, Renna (again like me) flubbed his line. The dialogue as written—and what I read in that auditorium—was: "You kill me, Smalls." Only during filming did it change to the iconic version when Renna misspoke during a take. It was, to put it simply, an error.

An error is both a subjective statistic peculiar to baseball and the bane of memory. And, as others have pointed out, such an error can disproportionately affect good players. To commit an error, one must have been in the right place at the right time, but the stat doesn't take that into account. So whereas I completely blew my audition—an error—baseball wouldn't give me credit for getting to that auditorium and giving it a shot. Paradoxically, Renna erred in reciting his lines, but it actually made the movie better. The error, after all, is what was remembered.

What if my greatest error is holding onto the memory of something that never happened?

My mother doesn't remember any of this audition. There is a possibility, remote though it may be, where I have misremembered everything. In this version, I was never there. I made it all up only after seeing *The Sandlot* in the theater. There are other errors, too.

The Sandlot, which I always remembered being a box office hit was not, in fact, a box office hit. Nineteen ninety-three was a stellar year for Hollywood. *Jurassic Park*, *The Fugitive*, *The Firm*, and *Sleepless in Seattle* each opened and together grossed nearly a billion dollars. *The Sandlot* didn't break $40 million. Even *Rookie of the Year*, another baseball film from that year, grossed almost twice as much as the feature film that was to have been my Hollywood debut. I remember nothing about *Rookie of the Year*.

Baseball is a sport that wants you to remember. Take the scorebook. A nineteenth-century invention, it allows fans to take notes about the game and thereby reconstruct each inning. Like chess notation, it's a blueprint for narrating a memory, a shared history. What it does not show— what it cannot show—is whether, for example, Babe Ruth called his shot in the legendary 1932 World Series or simply gestured to fans. That particular event, more magical than any pitch count, run, or error would have lived only in the subjective minds of the thousands of fans who were at Wrigley Field that day. The late Supreme Court Justice John Paul Stevens famously claimed to have been there as a twelve-year-old and said Ruth called his shot. I say the eleven-year-old version of me auditioned for *The Sandlot*. As far as I know, however, I'm the only one who remembers that.

The act of remembering is itself a kind of performance and, as such, subject to certain embellishments. When we perform memory, then, we open ourselves up to accessing not only a version of the truth but the ghosts of everything that's not. What I mean here, specifically, is nostalgia. Perhaps nostalgia itself is an error. An 18th-century neologism conjured from Greek, it means "a return home." The indefinite article "a" is key. How often do we find only one way home? Instead, the routes are sometimes clear, sometimes cluttered, and sometimes lies.

Sometimes we choose the path; sometimes the paths are chosen for us.

Just as *Rocky* isn't really about boxing, *The Sandlot* isn't really about baseball. A work of fiction, it's a frame story about a man recalling a version of his childhood. It drips with nostalgia for a time in his life that was fleeting and yet no less vivid. It's about moments of camaraderie and friendship set at precisely the moment in a young person's life when things are about to get physically and emotionally awkward. The characters in the movie, of course, don't know it yet.

But the rest of us do. And because we do, we look back at our own lives and dare to remember and misremember.

When I revisit this episode from my own childhood where I auditioned for a role as a baseball player, I know the game itself, ironically, had become performative for me. I was losing interest in the catching and the batting. In the 1993 season, I had a perfect fielding percentage— not one error—but only one measly hit. The players were getting bigger and more aggressive.

High school teams and scholarships were around the corner. But not for me. For me, 1993 will always be the year I quit baseball and the year I watched my Hollywood "career" flash before my eyes.

How strange it is, then, to think back to the ten minutes I spent in that auditorium and realize that some of those other kids were excited and enraptured by the experience of auditioning and the possibility of acting. It wouldn't surprise me to learn some of them have gone on to become performers in Los Angeles or community theater in cities around the country. They are the extras of my memories (protagonists of their own), who briefly entered my life faceless and exited the same. I know they don't remember me, but without them there that day, my experience somehow feels less meaningful, less shared.

Long after my purported audition, my family gathered to watch my mother's performance on *Walker, Texas Ranger*. The intro credits began rolling. Chuck Norris—superimposed over the Dallas skyline—Western hat, duster, carbine in hand, stoically looks off into the distance contemplating how he will take out that week's bad guys. We sat through the entire episode only to discover the producers had used a roundhouse kick to my mother's scene, leaving it on the floor with that week's villainy. But she still remembers Norris walking into the room. Or was she even there?

Q: Who won *The Twin Bill*'s 2024 Best Baseball Nonfiction Book?

A: Noah Gittell, *Baseball: The Movie*

Illustration by Mark Mosley

I need to talk to you about the time Torii Hunter stole a home run from Barry Bonds at the 2002 All-Star Game

By Terry Horstman

But first I need to tell you what I hate about the 2002 All-Star Game

I hate that the 2002 All-Star Game ended in a tie because that is all anyone seems to remember about it. As both the American League and National League managers breezed through their respective pitching staffs with the score knotted at 7–7, Major League Baseball Commissioner Bud Selig announced in the middle of the 11th inning that the game would end in a tie if the National League didn't get a run across the plate. They didn't, and it did, marking only the second time ever the Midsummer Classic ended without a winner, the first since 1961.

The 2003 All-Star Game started a run of 13 consecutive MLB All-Star games that determined which league's representative in the World Series would get home-field advantage. "This time it counts," read several taglines promoting the game. This ill-advised wrinkle of the game ultimately came to an end, but will forever serve as the official milestone marker of professional sports leagues attempting to 'save' their respective all-star games.

I hate that the 2002 All-Star Game ended in a tie because I hate that baseball's power brokers saw an opportunity to line their pockets with even more money by finding a way to turn a game that's supposed to be a celebration into a game that "counts." The eleven innings of the 2002 All-Star Game may not have decided a clear winner on the scoreboard at Miller Park in Milwaukee that day, but the play on the field was definitely a celebration of all the great things baseball is and can hope to be.

There were many great plays on the field, but I'm thinking of one play in particular.

Bottom of the 1st. Two outs. Nobody on. Boston Red Sox ace Derek Lowe on the mound, and San Francisco Giants' all-world slugger Barry Bonds at the plate looking at a 1-1 count. Bonds got a pitch he liked and smacked it to deep right-center, the ball surely destined for the soil beyond the outfield walls of Milwaukee's hitter-friendly yard.

The ball came close to touching down in home run territory, but it never got there. It's important to remember why. It's important to remember Minnesota Twins Torii Hunter was the man playing center field.

The Minnesota Twins: Get To Know 'Em!

I hate that the 2002 All-Star Game ended in a tie because I fucking hate Bud Selig, the commissioner who made the decision to call it a draw.

To truly understand the exploits of Torii Hunter playing center field in the 2002 All-Star Game, we need to first go back to the public perception of the Minnesota Twins before Opening Day in 2001. Not only had the team failed to reach the playoffs every single season since their iconic victory in the 1991 World Series, but they entered the 2001 season having eclipsed the 90-loss mark in each of the previous four years. The 'Metrodome Magic' that blessed the team on their way to World Series wins in '87 and '91 had long run dry, and contention for so much as a division championship appeared to be several years away.

Besides hardcore fans, many baseball-loving Minnesotans didn't know much about the Twins' opening day roster heading into the 2001 season. I sure didn't. I knew of guys like pitcher Brad Radke and outfielder Matt Lawton, each with one all-star appearance to their names and both were quality players as well as fan-favorites, but not franchise-altering superstars. The rest of the roster held the alluring possibility of potential synonymous with youth, but recognizable names were few and far between.

The Twins own promotional campaign for the 2001 season was literally punctuated with the tagline, "The Minnesota Twins: Get To Know 'Em!"

The language was as self-deprecating as it was self-aware. It didn't immediately cure fans of the inherent apathy from four years worth of nearly triple-digit losses, but the authenticity of the campaign played well locally. If the young Twinkies also played well, then it wouldn't be hard to imagine the Hubert H Humphrey Metrodome (the fucking worst stadium in baseball) packed, loud, and vibrant once again.

Also at play in 2001 was Bud Selig's infamous 'Contraction Plan.' As baseball's head honcho, Selig targeted the Twins and the Montreal Expos as prime candidates for contraction, a fancy word for 'erasure.' The move would eliminate the two franchises from Major League Baseball along with all the financial commitments that came with running professional baseball teams in the great sporting cities of Minneapolis and Montreal and award the owners of both teams with hefty buyouts.

On top of the recent spell of losing, there were a few other factors that made the Twins a particularly juicy, low-hanging fruit for Selig to exploit. The aforementioned Metrodome, a facility outdated by multiple decades before it even opened in 1982, was not exactly a summertime hotspot in the Twin Cities. The combination of bad baseball and even worse indoor conditions saw the Twins plunge to the bottom of the league attendance rankings. Whether the Twins could ever turn it around on the field, and secure funding for a new stadium off the field, apparently wasn't a project Selig had time for.

Geography also played a part in the deal. Selig, a Milwaukee product and owner of the Brewers before he became commissioner, would never admit it, but disposing of the Twins would create a massive hole for the availability of Major League Baseball in the Upper Midwest. If the Twins didn't exist, could baseball fans in Minnesota and the Dakotas adopt the Brewers as their own and make annual pilgrimages to Miller Park and pay homage to the statue of Bud Selig that stands outside its gates for love of the game and in the name of regional stewardship? Probably not, but who knows, Selig's work history with Minnesota's closest geographic competitor was impossible to ignore.

The owner of the Twins, Carl Pohlad, also reportedly wanted out of owning the club and would have made a hell of a lot more money in a contraction buyout than he would have by continuing to own the team. All Pohlad ever did was proclaim that "no one wants to keep baseball in Minnesota more than I," and then embark on another plan that directly involved the Twins leaving Minnesota. An unsuccessful attempt to sell the team in 1997 to North Carolina businessman Don Beaver, who would have moved the team to the Winston-Salem area, was barely out of the rearview mirror by the time contraction talks came up and Selig owed Pohlad a favor from when Tempus Investment Corp., a company controlled by Pohlad, lent the Brewers $3 million in 1995. A dark time in baseball when many clubs were scrambling for money in the wake of the 1994 players' strike.

Loans between owners and clubs were explicitly forbidden by Major League Baseball's own rules, but the owners were never going to agree to punish their own billionaire brethren. Nothing came of the sleazy and nefarious business dealings between Pohlad and Selig, and by the time 2001 rolled around, contraction was officially on the books and both Selig and the league had all but led the Twins and the Expos to baseball's gallows.

By the end of 2001, the owners voted in favor of contraction by a vote of 28–2. The dissenting votes of course cast by the ownership of the Twins and the Expos, with Pohlad meaninglessly putting his name on the right side of history on paper after years of actively trying to ensure professional baseball in the North Star State met its demise.

Had the owners got their way, the Twins and Expos would have disappeared like a baseball pitched to Barry Bonds up in the zone. The players on both teams would likely have gone into a pool to be divvied up among the remaining 28 teams in some kind of sick, twisted, reverse expansion draft. Sports owners usually do get their way too. They are the first ones presented with the championship trophy after championship victories for reasons beyond any rational thinking human. But they didn't get their way this time. Pushback from the Major League Baseball Players Association and a court injunction that ruled the Twins must honor their lease, which called for at least one more season at the Metrodome, stifled their plans and the contraction dreams of the game's greediest and sleaziest individuals ultimately crumbled. The number of teams in the league would remain at 30, and the Twins would remain in Minnesota for at least one more season under the Dome's off-white Teflon sky.

Here's what no one predicted: the 2001 Twins were fucking good.

This is an essay about the 2002 All-Star Game, and 2002 is of course the year of the Moneyball Oakland A's, and everyone who's seen *Moneyball* knows the role that another very good Twins team played in that story, but it's impossible to talk about the 2002 All-Star Game, the 2002 Twins, Torii Hunter, or even Barry freaking Bonds in 2002, without first mentioning the incredible ride of the 2001 Twins.

The team's plea for Minnesotans to come out to the Metrodome to check out the Twins and 'Get To Know 'Em,' worked. Fans flocked to the Metrodome for its balmy indoor April weather, 'Dome Dogs,' and iconic Malt Cups (as much as the Dome sucked, it never gets enough credit for the concessions, which were always on point) and the Twins rewarded the fans by standing alone in first place in the AL Central. *Sports Illustrated* responded to the Twinkies' hot start by putting Matt Lawton on the cover of the magazine with the headline, 'Do You Believe in Miracles? All the first-place Twins have to do is hang on for another six months.'

No one takes summers for granted in Minnesota. After a long cold winter, and after a long and impossible-to-predict spring that often qualifies as second winter, summer in the North Star State is a gift as cherished as it is fleeting. While kids in other cities got to spend their summers at ballparks under the sky and stars, watching the game they loved played by players they loved even more, a breeze in their hair and a progressing sunburn on their skin; we Minneapolis kids had to choose. It was either the summer breeze, or watching the Twins in climate-controlled AC. The feel of natural grass under bare feet, or starting at astroturf dyed neon green so bright it hurt your eyes. Beach chairs in the sand, or plastic blue seats nailed into a cement cavern that didn't even face the right direction.

Willingly spending your approximate eight minutes of summer inside to watch baseball in a miserable structure that wasn't even designed for baseball is a *choice*. It was a choice that could not be defended when it also meant watching most of the Twins teams of my childhood, but by the time the 2001 team came around, a team affectionately known to me as 'The Contraction Kids,' the choice became a formality. Summertime sun could wait, the Metrodome and our first-place team was a'calling!

An absolutely stacked team in Cleveland eventually caught up to Minnesota and took that season's AL Central crown, but with 85 wins, three all-stars, and unmeasurable untapped potential, the Twins sent a message to the rest of Major League Baseball. Contraction be damned, the team was young, fun, and full of talent. Lawton teamed with Hunter and Jacque Jones to form the self-proclaimed 'Soul Patrol' outfield and were routinely featured in the 'Web Gems' segment of *Baseball Tonight* on ESPN. The team used the No. 1 pick in that year's MLB Draft in June on hometown catching prodigy Joe Mauer (who turned out to be pretty good, you betcha!). Lightning-fast shortstop Cristian Guzmán led the league in triples for a second consecutive year and earned his first All-Star appearance. Starting pitchers Joe Mays and Eric Milton earned their first All-Star selections as well and teamed up with Radke to give the Twins one of the most solid rotations in all of baseball. They may not have won the division or made the playoffs, but at the end of the season and on the brink of erasure, the 2001 Minnesota Twins gave Twins' fans everywhere something they hadn't had since the release of *Little Big League* in 1994; a reason to believe, and the team's promotional campaign eventually changed from "Get To Know 'Em" to "Gotta See 'Em."

A small statistical footnote: Hunter led the Twins in homers in 2001 with 27, the same year Bonds broke the all-time record with 73.

Nothing but Raindrops

After we got to know 'em, it didn't take long for us to learn to love 'em and perhaps no member of that era of Twins baseball was more popular than Torii Hunter, who earned Gold Glove honors for the first time in 2001 and repeated as a Gold Glover every single season for the rest of the decade. No. 48 in your programs, No. 1 in your hearts, and an F8 on your scorecard every time a baseball was hit in his general direction.

I hate that the 2002 All-Star Game ended in a tie because it certainly would not have ended in a tie if anyone other than Torii Hunter were playing center field for the American League in the first inning. I hate that, but still, I love that the 2002 All-Star Game was played in Milwaukee, because although his Contraction plan had been all but foiled at that point, Selig still had not received suitable comeuppance for what he tried to do to the Twinkies (he still hasn't, if we're being honest), and I love that the American League's starting center fielder at the All-Star Game in Selig's hometown, in a stadium that has a statue of Selig himself in front of it, and on Selig's old field, took the field in the Twins' classy pin-striped away grays with 'Minnesota' across his chest.

All of this was on my 14-year-old mind in the middle of the summer in 2002. My beloved Twinkies avoided erasure, but were still seeking their first playoff appearance since 1991. A team that often lost 94 games a year, I did not yet know the end of this season would bring the taste of 94 wins and the first AL Central title of my lifetime. I did not yet know the run they would make would conjure spirits of a World Series run I was old enough to be alive for but too young to remember. I was aware of another pretty good small-market and low-payroll team in Oakland, even if I was not yet aware of the term 'Moneyball,' but I did not yet know a book would be written about the how and the why of their goodness and that their historic winning streak would come to an end at the hands of my beloved Twinkies and that their championship dreams would also come to an end at the hands of my beloved Twinkies. I did not yet know about the Hollywood film that would come out about that team 10 years later, and in that film, the Twins would serve as the ultimate villains (even though the Yankees are truly the ultimate villains, in any story really), but the filmmakers would also change Game 5 at the Coliseum from a day game to a night game and they would also make Eddie Guardado more jacked than Jose Canseco.

I just knew my favorite baseball team still had the right to exist and the young man patrolling center field for my favorite baseball team was a human highlight reel, roaming the warning track with a glove touched by the gods that had a chance to snag any ball that wasn't leaving this planet.

Entering the 2002 All-Star Game, Barry Bonds had only hit one home run in his 10 previous All-Star appearances. His pace in 2002 was far short of the 73 bombs he hit the year prior, but still flirted with the league lead. He finished the year 11 shy of Alex Rodriguez's MLB-leading 57 homers, but still took home the second of his eventual four consecutive National League MVP honors.

Bonds thought he opened the scoring of the 2002 All-Star Game when he connected with Lowe's pitch. I'm sure Bud Selig watching from the stuffy confines of his old owner's box thought so too. I'm sure just about everyone in the stands at Miller Park thought he did, Joe Buck and Tim McCarver calling the game for Fox thought he did, and Ichiro Suzuki playing right field for the American League definitely thought he did. Everyone watching the game thought Bonds' blast to right center field was gone.

I should amend that to: *almost* everyone watching the game thought it was a home run. Twins fans watching the game saw Torii track it, attack it, and knew it was a different kind of 'no-doubter.'

The catch itself was incredible, if a tad pedestrian by Torii Hunter standards. He timed the jump perfectly, went up with his glove hand, and calmly plucked the ball from the other side of infinity and brought it back inside the ballpark. Ichiro, who had the best view, just smiled. Hunter clearly wanted to smile too, but tried to suppress at first, as if robbing a God of a home run was a daily occurrence. He kept his cool for a second, but after an encouraging shove from Ichiro, the enormity of what he'd just done, of who he'd just denied, took over and the 25-year-old from Pine Bluff, Arkansas burst into laughter as he jogged back towards the infield with the ball tucked into his glove.

But the best part of the moment by far was the reaction of Bonds. The best player on the planet looked shocked for a moment, then as he slowed his trot between first and second, just smiled and shook his head. He jogged towards Hunter, went in for a high-five, and then wrapped his arms around him and lifted him off the ground and above his shoulders. There was nothing more than respect intended by

Bonds in the playful embrace, but there was still something significant in it; Bonds playing in his 11th All-Star Game lifting up Hunter playing in his first. Arguably the greatest player of all time literally and figuratively doing more to lift up our franchise than any of the league's perfumed bureaucrats at Rockefeller Center ever did. The Minnesota Twins had already turned the page away from losing and extinction towards sustainability and winning, but it wasn't until the 2002 All-Star Game that the arrival of their new era was announced to the world. Minnesotans should always be grateful to Barry Bonds for the part he played in the moment.

In his very next at-bat, Bonds blasted one to the upper deck in right field. Much deeper, and much, much further to right field than his first. A fair ball crushed to a spot as far away from Hunter as possible. I have no problem interpreting that as another sign of respect from the game's all-time home run leader, though I still hate that the 2002 All-Star Game ended in a tie, I'll always love Barry for that.

Every time I make the 335-mile drive from Minneapolis to Milwaukee and watch the Twins or any other team play the Brewers at their great ballpark once known as Miller Park, I always take a minute to gaze out to the wall in right-center. As soon as I find the exact spot, I replay Torii's picturesque robbery of Bonds in my mind and smile. I trace his steps after the catch to the outskirts of the infield where Bonds was there to greet him, tease him, hug him, and toss him, and just laugh. Every single time. I never forget to take a moment for one of my favorite moments when I find myself in the stadium that held the 2002 All-Star Game.

And I never, ever forget to say "Go fuck yourself, Bud. Contract this!" when I walk past that damn statue on my way in and out of the stadium that held the 2002 All-Star Game.

Q: What sports lit journal does Terry Horstman edit?

A: *The Under Review*

Illustration by Jason David Córdova

Steve Perry Pinch-Hits for Steve Perry
By Aarik Danielsen

In the even-numbered years of our Lord, the Giants stretched the sky from San Francisco in all cardinal directions, to my Midwest and beyond. Every win rippled the canopy, transmitting bay air and birdsong on a line to my satisfied senses.

Permit me and I'll supply a primer on the players, plot the twists of each World Series club. But my favorite mid-inning stretch outlives all the dynasty thrills; I reconstruct it from memory and TV static at least once a week.

Journey's "Lights" plays over the PA, as always. But one night, the golden tablets of ballpark tradition fracture and a TV camera pans up to Steve Perry, former rock deity. Dressed in black with hair of the selfsame color draping his shoulders, he might be the Steve Perry of 1979 or 1984. Only older folds of skin give him away—only this, and his posture.

Singing along, aloud with the words he etched into musical lore, he appears guileless in public for perhaps the first time. His body knows how to accentuate each note like a frontman does, giving the melody true voice. Yet he seems to relax into the confines of Section 219, cooler than any spotlight.

At first I embraced the easy read: bemused has-been caught up in playing to whoever or whatever's left. But stop and take this brief test, one I've given myself.

Bow your head and close your eyes—like a prayer, go on. Now lift, now open. Can you picture Foreigner's Lou Gramm crooning "Double Vision" after a Mets 6-4-3? Or Kevin Cronin of REO Speedwagon unable to "fight this feeling anymore" from the club seats at Wrigley Field? Not without prejudice.

Steve Perry sings, and he looks every bit the natural. A man born to do something the way Lincecum was born to rock the rubber back and forth. The way Sergio Romo was made by God to stare, then throw sliders. Everything Steve Perry sings is a little too much and just the right amount. Forever caring more than you or me, but forever teaching us to care.

What notes stick in a great singer's head? Maybe divorced from his former mates, Steve Perry feels free to raise his voice in the absence of glances heavy with the freight of decades.

Maybe that mournful catch just around the bridge is gospel: it really is sad—oh!—those mornings out on the road without San Francisco, without its every charm. Here, swept into its center, he knows what everything's worth. The city rising up around him is the thing. The Giants are the thing. This moment, *weightless together*, is the thing.

Just minutes before the next first batter, maybe Steve Perry counts up all the Mondays and Thursdays gone forever, all those highway runs. Doing the math of poets and icons, he knows singing one song on one night covers the sin of a few days away.

Who am I to judge the shape redemption takes? Maybe ribs swell, pressing hard and beautiful against your skin, whenever 41,000 people sing your song without turning the microphone their way to beam "Sing, San Francisco!"

My God, stay pure, Steve Perry. Triumph comes so soon for your Giants. And transfiguration comes whenever a man is most himself between the very lights he created.

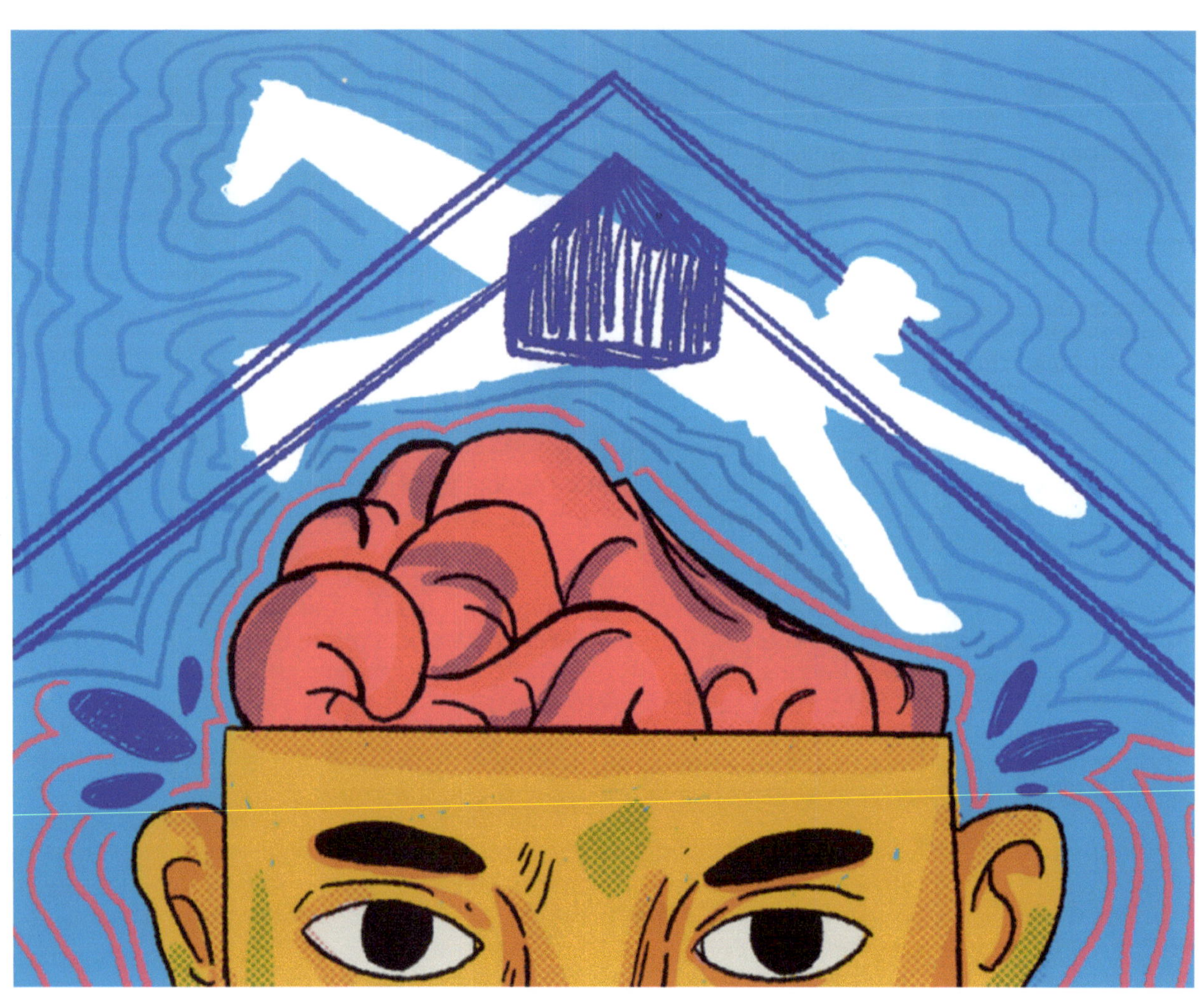

Illustration by Elliot Lin

Oligo My Own
By Eligio Mares

I rounded third base with a vengeance. Once this was said and done, once the dust settled, one thing was for certain, my life would never be the same ever again. A league of my own. Oligo, my own.

No way I was going around him, I was going through him! The competitive force had already decided for me. Middle School P.E. Pickup baseball on pick-up loop. White lines on hard asphalt. The only thing that stood between me and home was the biggest guy in the entire school.

I wasn't even supposed to be there! This class was for outcasts, future stoners, stoner musicians, musicians. Yet there I was, no talent but baseball, no rhythm but running. This was my stage and I was determined to shine. Stride. Wide. Pride. Big Mike had no chance!

Big Mike was a guitarist turned catcher, at least for that hour. The only thing banging would be heads, as rigidly as the rock he riffed. The play came in from the center field band hall, ball as soft as brain, cracks and crevices and all. Music. Emotion. Material. Grunge. Grudge. Sponge.

I started to play organized baseball three years prior. Initially, my parents were apprehensive. To them, there was a very thin line between win and sin, as thin as the imaginary chalk line that marks foul play on a middle school bus loop. Nonexistent.

Unfair ball. Sin, and lose.

Together in seventh grade, now eighth. It was The Musicians vs. The Mexicans, a band of brothers against brothers. I felt Coach O. sided with them, getting all the calls, I thought. My parent's cult, the coach's insult all came to a head and my head was about to pay the price.

The final stretch of our imaginary diamond ran semi-diagonally to West Eagle, a two-way drive that separates the school from the county medical center. I would end up at that center seven years later, but for now the only thing that mattered was a frustration run up on the board.

The irony is that dad didn't like the brutal presentation of football, yet there I laid flat on my back, next to Big Mike, swimming in a pool of regret, staring, praying at the clear sky God that didn't want me playing baseball to begin with. No pain, no gain, all migraine.

It would otherwise be a pretty good school year. I built a small CO_2 car in woodshop, peeked at a Penthouse or two, and became the only Ben Franklin on stage at Science Place, kite high and bifocals low. My vision would never be a concern, 20/20 still in 2020, but my occipital lobe would.

The bottom right corner of the band hall squarely marked straight away center field. On the other side of the building, down a small hill, there was a leveling of the ground, making way for a brand new high school baseball field. Up to that point, they had been using a city park.

The corner of West Eagle Drive and Deer Park Road was the future site of the new field, just in time for my freshman year of high school. The following year, I received Newcomer of the Year honors. But middle school sponge ball does not care about America's favorite pastime, nor about the future.

The time was now! Plowing full speed ahead, clearing way, clearing path. I don't remember any of the other players or their positions. I don't remember the batter or the fielder fielding the ball like Dad fielded asparagus in the hot fields of Walla Walla, Washington's deep past.

I was coming in from second and all I cared about was being first. Me, myself, and Big Mike, a fellow classmate that, despite being there since second grade, I knew very little about. We never spoke in class, high school, or since. I hear he's lost a lot of weight and looks unrecognizable.

117

The one thing I did know about Big Mike, aside from his rock guitar exploits, was that he also played on the school's marching band, practicing in the very hall that basically represented the upper deck in our street stadium. He played the baby tuba with the big mouth.

The wide lip opening of the baritone resembled the CT scan I would have to slide into seven years later, headfirst, like sliding decisively into home plate, ramming into heavy metal solo barricade. RBI now, MRI later. Pressure. Baritone. Barricade. Barometric.

I am not even sure what the call was at the plate, or if it even matters at this juncture of life. I wonder if it was clear-cut, as black and white as the surface we stomped on. Or did it fall within the gray matter of the brain? The cynical me thinks they got the call yet again.

The experienced teacher in me now thinks that Coach O. actually rooted for me. If he didn't give me any of the calls, it was because he was trying to level the playing field, just like the leveling of the baseball grounds down below, a year away from the varsity team up above.

From a family of boxers, I played a blue-collar style of game. Baseball, and eventually basketball in high school, a dual sport threat like Michael Jordan. Broken battle.

Cracked cranium. Bleeding brain. I wanted to be big like Mike, but on this day, I did not want to be Big Mike.

After high school, I would go on to take up employment at a blue-collar plant on the other side of town. As quickly as I rounded third, I went from first-string athlete to second-shift operator. "Down in a Hole" as my grunge anthem, I thought my playing days were officially over.

In the midst of my two-and-a-half-year tenure on the evening shift, I was recruited to play on the company's softball team. A group of men with great intentions, soberly competitive during the early morning games of Saturday tournaments, victims of a brunch cocktail of booze, boos, lose.

I was the only one not on the first shift to play on the team. My supervisor ordered me out back to practice with the guys on Wednesdays. On the clock. Compensated. Conflict of interest. No complaints. At seven dollars per hour, three hours a week, I was officially a paid athlete.

Now on the day shift, that same supervisor pulled me off the floor yet again. He ordered me outback, straight into town to see my family physician, Dr. Alling. Ailing. Present confusion. Future confession. Past concussion. It had caught up to me, like rounding third with a vengeance, and I had no defense.

Mares is my last name. It means oceans. Seas. I try to stem the Tide. Wide. Pride. I often think about eighth grade. Education. Physical. I wonder how I would have called that one play if I had been the umpire. I am not really sure, but I think it's safe to say that I was not safe at all.

The letter 'g' in my name Eligio is soft. The 'g' in my diagnosis hits double hard. Oligodendroglioma. The term so technical it runs like a long double deep in the gap of a dark MRI tube. I rounded third, ran straight into the medical center across the street. This time, taking the long way home.

Q: What prize was this piece nominated for?
A: Pushcart Prize

"Meet the" Vignettes
Eligio Mares

Who are you?

A public school teacher with 15 years experience, specializing in Bilingual Education K-12th grade, currently on medical disability for an Oligodendroglioma brain tumor. I grew up in a rural town in north Texas, currently living in a suburb of Dallas.

What was the inspiration for your piece?

I was inspired to write this piece after a recent trip to the Oligo Nation Gala in Manhattan and the Cooperstown Hall of Fame.

What's your favorite team?

Texas Rangers

Who is your favorite player?

The Professor, Greg Maddux, for his methodical approach to the game.

What's your favorite baseball memory?

Serving as team captain in high school.

What's the highlight of your writing career?

I was nominated for the Pushcart Prize.

Favorite baseball book? Movie?

My favorite baseball book is *Daybreak at Chavez Ravine: Fernandomania and the Remaking of the Los Angeles Dodgers* by Erik Sherman. My favorite baseball documentary is *30 for 30: Jordan Rides the Bus.*

Q: How many people contributed to the anthology?

A: 71

Illustration by Matt Lawrence

Camden Yards
By John Schmidtke

July 30, 1993

I think the ball slipped out of Scott Cooper's hand. Mo Vaughn at first base didn't even try to jump; he stood with his right foot loosely toeing the bag and watched the ball sail over his head.

"Heads up," I said to our boys, my voice sharp with warning. "Ball coming!"

***

God invented baseball for July afternoons with the temperature in the mid-80s and a light wind blowing out to left just enough to keep the flags awake. We were testing God's invention as part of our family's summer trip from Hawaii to the East Coast. The goal was to see as many of Mary's eight sisters as we could in a two-week vacation. Two sisters lived in Baltimore and we decided to spend a Friday afternoon at a game between the Orioles and the visiting Boston Red Sox. The usher had just wiped off our third-row seats in Section 14. The seats faced shallow right field barely past the infield cut. Mary was already sitting down.

I still stood, watching the Red Sox take infield practice: Cooper at third, John Valentin at short, Scott Fletcher at second, Vaughn at first, and Tony Pena behind the plate. A coach hit fungo to each fielder. A grounder to the fielder's left, the catch, the gather, the throw to first, and then a grounder to the fielder's right, the catch, the gather, and the throw to first again, and again, and again; a rhythmic cycle of grace, agility, and power. Vaughn's glove popped with each throw. As the infielders worked on the diamond, the boys stood next me wearing their Hawaii Kai All-Star hats—Scott, 10, with his glove on, and Riley, 8, carrying his glove under his armpit. They stared around the nearly new stadium—it had opened the season before—at the retro-design, the brick walls, the iron supports, and the green seats filling with the crowd. They looked for Cal Ripken Jr. in the Orioles' dugout. They didn't look at the field.

I watched the Boston coach swing and hit a sharp two-hopper to Cooper's far right, forcing him to backhand the ball in foul territory and to leap, wheel, and throw to first while in the air. That's when the ball slipped out of his hand and sailed over Mo Vaughn's head.

You can't appreciate the power of a major leaguer's arm unless you've been close to the field. TV doesn't capture the deadly speed and air-ripping hiss of a well-thrown ball, and radio only hints at the force of the ball with the distant slap of leather on leather lost behind the announcer's voice. My words made the boys look up, the bills of both their hats pointing at the infield, and when they looked up they saw a well-thrown ball by a major leaguer tearing the air their way.

Every baseball fan comes to the ballpark hoping to take home a ball as a souvenir. The one that might be ours came at us in a rush. From where I stood, I knew I couldn't make the play without moving hard to my right and maybe knocking down one or both boys. As good as they were as fielders, I wasn't sure either of them could catch a ball thrown at major-league speed.

***

Our Scott has soft, sure hands. As a youth-league catcher he received the ball with nonchalant grace—very few passed balls. As a first baseman he turned lots of poor throws into outs. His first word as a baby had been "ball." Mary and I played catch with him using tennis balls when he was five and six. When I took him to Kokohead District Park to try out for Pinto baseball as a seven-year-old, I walked him from the parking lot to the Pinto field feeling confident yet nervous. I knew he was good, but this was his first time throwing and catching in public.

The Pinto League coaches stood on the infield holding clipboards and stopwatches as they looked over the newcomers. The dads leaned on the chain-link fence near right field to watch their sons. The simple try-out started with the kids sprinting from home to first, one after the other. The coaches timed the sprints. Next, the boys lined up on the foul line and one at a time took a defensive stance at first base, glove ready. The Pinto division director rolled the ball from home to first. Every ball rolled smoothly. Every ball rolled right to the fielder. The boy at first base was supposed to field the ball and then throw to a coach near the pitcher's mound. Scott stood in the middle of the line of about thirty kids. I waited for his turn with confidence.

The ball from the Pinto director went through the first boy's legs. He turned, ran into right field, picked the ball up when it stopped rolling, and then heaved it toward second base rather than at the coach near the pitcher's mound. The Pinto coaches wrote notes on their clipboards. I smiled, knowing Scott could field rolled balls easily and knowing he could snap off a throw to the coach's chest. The second kid did the same as the first: he missed the ball, waited for it to stop rolling, picked it up, and threw wildly, with no attempt at accuracy. Each kid did the same. Knowing what I knew, I saw Scott as a potential number one draft pick. I stood shoulder to shoulder with the other dads. I prepared to stay calm, to not react to Scott's play, not wanting to show off when it was my stud kid's turn. I knew Scott would look the ball into his glove, scoop the ball to his chest, turn his shoulder to his target, crow hop once, and throw the ball on line to the coach.

When his turn came, Scott took his stance. The Pinto director rolled the ball. Scott watched the ball roll between his legs. I'm sure I straightened up from the fence and gasped—what was that? Scott ran after the ball and waited for it to stop. I paced behind the other dads. Whose kid was that? Scott threw towards second and the ball rolled into left field. I turned away. What in the…? The coaches on the field wrote notes on their clipboards.

"Next!" the director called. Scott jogged off the field towards me, smiling.

Keeping my voice casual, I said, "Hey, Buddy. Have fun?"

"Yeah!"

I kept disappointment out of my question. "Were you nervous?"

"No! It was fun."

Don't be that dad, I thought, even as I asked, "Did the ball take a funny bounce?"

"No."

Leave it on the field, John. Don't take it home. Don't be that dad. "Was it too hard?"

"No."

I couldn't help myself. "What happened?"

"Huh?"

I had to know, "The ball got through your legs. What happened?"

"Nothing."

I was all in. "Nothing?" I asked. "How'd it get through your legs?"

Scott looked at me like I was stupid.

"It was supposed to."

"Huh?"

"We all did it that way, Dad."

As Scott Cooper's errant throw screamed across the Camden Yards infield, I wondered whether our Scott would make the play this time.".

***

But maybe the ball was headed for Riley; it had a slight hook as it closed on us. All year in the regular season, and in the post-season All-Stars, Riley had played third—the hot corner they call it in the Bigs, but it's just a tepid position at the Pinto level: no seven- or eight-year-old ever yanked a screamer down the left field line. Certainly nothing like the fungo Cooper backhanded in Camden Yards' foul territory. Riley's hands weren't as soft as Scott's, but he stopped everything hit his way, knocked down anything he didn't catch cleanly, and made the play with a powerful, high-elbowed throw. But even if his glove had been on his hand rather than under his arm, I had no confidence he could catch Scott Cooper's ball.

***

In the slow instant after I said "heads up," I decided to try for the ball. I looked down, like a first baseman finding the bag, to see whether I could scoot quickly to my right without knocking the boys down and hurting them. But I knew I was coming their way no matter what—a bruise from falling against a seat or a scrape on the knee from skidding on the concrete would hurt or bleed, but getting beaned could be deadly. When I looked down, I saw I couldn't scoot to my right at all. Both boys were on their knees and elbows like supplicants begging mercy, butts up, hands over their heads, the bills of their All-Star hats touching the floor, their gloves on the concrete next to them, and both using the seats of Row Two as a shield.

Scott Cooper's errant throw crunched into the back of the seat in front of our Scott. Two inches higher and it would have cleared that seat in Row Two and smacked into Riley's seatback. No way either boy would have caught it. I might have, even barehanded, but it would've hurt. Scott Cooper's ball ricocheted down from the seatback and into the spring-loaded seat itself. The force of the ricochet pushed the Row Two seat down and the seat's springs absorbed the energy of the throw. As the springs pulled the seat up and into place, the ball softly flipped straight up. Our MLB souvenir gently floated at chest level, harmless, waiting.

***

The best in the ballpark showed off at Camden Yards that day. Mo Vaughn might not have been able to catch Scott Cooper's pre-game throw, but in the third inning he jacked a two-run home run. Two years later, Vaughn would hit .300 with 39 homers and be recognized as the American League MVP. Harold Baines, the Orioles' Designated Hitter, crushed a two-out grand slam in the fourth inning. He hit .313 that year. In his 22-year career, the six-time All-Star would drive in more runs than anyone not in the Baseball Hall of Fame. Andre Dawson, the Red Sox DH, the 1977 Rookie of the Year, an eight-time All-Star, the 1987 National League MVP, and a future Hall of Famer, cranked a three-run homer in the first. And the best on the field, Cal Ripken, Jr., a 19-time All-Star, a two-time MVP, the 1982 Rookie of the Year, the holder of the most consecutive games played in the history of baseball (2,632), and another member of the Hall of Fame, went deep with a solo shot in the second.

But none of them—not Vaughn, not Baines, not Dawson, and not Ripken—caught a ball when the springs of the seat in Row Two flipped it softly in the air. None of their sons, All-Star hats askew, looked up at them from the concrete. None of their sons looked up at them with wide eyes showing a mix of fear, relief, and wonder to see their dad unexpectedly holding a major league baseball. None of their sons thought the ball had been caught barehanded on the fly. And none of their wives looked at them with raised eyebrows that said, "I know what you're thinking. Have your fun for a second—I know you can't help yourself—but you ought to tell your sons the truth."

God invented baseball for families to enjoy on a July afternoon, the air in the mid-80s and a light wind blowing out to left just enough to make memories.

Q: .406 Press published this book. Who has the highest average since Ted Williams hit .406?

A: Tony Gwynn, .394

Illustration by Elliot Lin

Fiction

Illustration by Jason David Córdova

Rickey Henderson Sits by a Lake

By Brendan Gillen

MAY 1, '91. A'S. YANKS. Bottom of the fourth. Rickey Henderson steals third, swipes Lou Brock's record from the books, yanks the bag out of the dirt, and holds it aloft like sacrament, the Bay gray sky glinting off his wraparound shades. He clutches a mic, and with his mother, Brock himself and forty-thousand in green and gold bearing witness, is swept up in the moment, issues eight words that will chase him forever: *Today, I am the greatest of all time.*

Everyone knows this part.

What if we don't know the rest?

What if, after the game, Rickey Henderson doesn't go home. Doesn't kiss his wife goodnight or tuck his three little daughters into bed. Steers a forest green Eddie Bauer past his glittering condo with regret searing his lips. Keeps the radio off because his thoughts are loud. What if he already knows they'll twist his words? *The greatest of all time? Where does he get off?* Make him sound cocky. Arrogant. Crazy. Shit, they already poke fun at him for referring to himself in the third person. What if he's always done this to admonish himself, because he cares so much? *Rickey, what the hell you doing chasing a two-one slider?* What if they simply asked?

What if Rickey Henderson steers his truck south on the 580, cuts east to Chabot Park in the purple twilight. Kills the engine and takes a deep breath, unclips his seatbelt. Gets out and walks towards the lip of the lake, hears the cicadas sing, a sound not unlike high heat whizzing past his ear. What if in the distance there's a golf course where he sometimes plays, even though he hates the sport, because when everything in your life is fast, you have to force yourself into a lower gear. What if he finds a bench and sits down, listens to the lake lap the shore, a liquid metronome. Counts the precious seconds in his head. Two-point-nine: the time it takes for him to steal second with a good jump. Three-point-one: the average pitcher-catcher throw out attempt. What if he told them about this? What if he told them about the stopwatch in his locker, the graph paper with the pencil scratch. The hours of game film, breaking down wind-ups. Would it make a difference? Change the narrative? Would he find himself sitting on a bench by a lake in the fading light, mouthing the words, feeling their familiar shape? *Today, I am the greatest of all time.* What if he's been saying these words every day for as long as he can remember? What if today there just happened to be a microphone? What if his mother—who gave birth to him on Christmas day in the back of an Oldsmobile— once told him, *If you don't believe it, nobody will?*

What if they knew what Rickey knows? That they could say it too, that all it takes is a little courage.

What if, the night after he makes history, Rickey Henderson stands up from a park bench with a clear head, walks back to his truck, gets in, and fires the engine. Merges back onto the freeway, lowers the windows, feels the cool spring air rush in. Begins to gain speed: seventy, eighty, ninety. What if the speedometer nips three digits, not because he feels free, but because he's already leaving those eight words behind. What if the what-ifs don't matter? What if this is just the beginning? What if a smile begins to take shape on Rickey Henderson's lips as he realizes something that will have the rest of the league chasing his shadow: if the words can't catch him, nothing can.

Q: Who published the most short stories in *The Twin Bill*?
A: Lauren McNulty, four

Watercolor by Michaela Paulson

The Life of Birds
By Peter Matthiessen Wheelwright

IN THE STUDY AND CLASSIFICATION OF BIRDS there seems to have developed some confusion about the Baltimore Oriole. At least, it seems that way to Ben. Recently, while conducting his field trips, he has begun to feel awkward in his presentation of the Oriole. Although he knows what he is talking about, something is not right. He has been feeling that either he is not saying what he knows or that some relevant news, which would change everything and whose coming he is vaguely aware of, has not yet reached him.

Ben is an amateur ornithologist and feels most comfortable with scientific method—or, at least, his version of it. He is willing to provide a reasonable allowance for other forms of considering the world's phenomena, but his tolerance of these alternatives is easily exhausted by even the mildest whiff of *metaphysical* speculation. Indeed, a lack of logical principle and scientific reasoning usually provokes in him a burst of indignant pedantry for which he is famous, avoided, and, of late, somewhat sorry.

Ben developed his interest in birds as the director of a small New England wildlife sanctuary set in the center of a small New England town. The 100-acre sanctuary was the bequest of one of the town's founding fathers who, having transformed three thousand acres of forest into a small commuter village, acquired a change of mind during his final days. Convinced that his de-forestation had deprived the community of its entire oxygen supply, he departed this life gasping for air with his lungs in perfect working order.

The sanctuary is comprised mostly of hardscrabble rock, pin oaks, shadbark hickory, and patches of "poverty" grass. Emerging like a tumescent fungus from the domestic grid of well-arranged lawns, its modest acreage hosts only a scanty coterie of birds, squirrels, and a few expatriate wilderness creatures such as The Northern Raccoon, whose evolved nature is to hunker down within the ring of garbage cans surrounding this largely lifeless woodland. The Audubon Society declined sponsorship.

There is no real staff at the sanctuary other than Ben, and his primary function there is to run the gift shop which sits by the road at the sanctuary's entrance. This task is not unimportant since most visitors are usually casually lost motorists whose need to get anywhere is not urgent and whose attention is easily diverted to the shop's abundant ceramic wildlife.

Occasionally, however, Ben is called upon to lead field trips for small groups of bird watchers.

He enjoys doing this; it affords him the opportunity to exercise his position as a man of the natural sciences. On these narrated walks through the sanctuary, Ben will typically provide a detailed lecture on the birds they might be expected to see and, after their walk, a brief discussion on why they had not seen them. But no one seems to leave disappointed, least of all Ben. His analytical rendering of birdlife never seems to require…well, actual birdlife. Good science is like that, he says.

Nevertheless, recently, it was in these woods that, while speaking of the Baltimore Oriole, Ben first noticed a feeling of odd anticipation— something imminent and unsettling—as if the sanctuary itself was poised to fold inside out, swapping the center for periphery and forcing the small town to suddenly hew its fragile civilization from inside nature's hard heart.

It began like this.

"You will know the Oriole as a brilliant orange or yellow bird with black and white markings displayed on the wings and head," he said, "Its voice is the sweetest of North American birds…a wonderful thing to hear but, unfortunately, a difficult voice to trace, lilting as it does from within the dense upper canopy of the bird's nesting tree. The Oriole, unlike its close relative The American Crow, prefers its distance and its alluring song is but a false promise."

Its alluring song is but a false promise…?!

Ben had surprised himself. He had offered this lyrical description to the group as if he were laying the bird itself into their palms. It was unlike him. He grew silent, worried that continuing with any further ornitho-logical analysis might cause the bird to fly out of their cupped hands in some oddly altered and unexplainable state.

And then it happened.

One of the birdwatchers, with innocent charm and lethal misconception, remarked on his familiarity with the "Baltimore" Oriole. "Oh yes, the Baaawl…timore Oriole; that *is* a lovely bird and, you know, there is a baseball team named for that bird – just like the St. Louis Cardinals and that Canadian team, what is it? – The Toronto Blue Jays. Yes, of course, except those aren't real birds. Right, Ben? There's no St. Looois…Cardinal; it's just a plain Red Cardinal, isn't that right?"

Ben experienced a mild loss of balance. At first, he thought he might have been holding his breath too long – something he had found himself doing more and more while looking through his binoculars. But, he also knew that this birdwatcher had stumbled into an important matter in need of sorting out.

Centering himself again, Ben responded with a nod and a good-natured *ain't-life-grand-and-that-little-observation-proves-it* chuckle that he was only partially convinced would prevent a recurring loss of foothold. He began speaking while trying to figure out just what it was that he wanted to say.

"Actually, there is no such thing as the "Baltimore" Oriole as we know it," he said.

How did we ever get this news?

"Until recently, the eastern version of this bird, the so-called…Baltimore Oriole…

Why Baltimore?

"…was thought to be a different species from the western version, the so-called Bullock's Oriole…

Who is Bullock?! Did he give us this news? Why?

"…However, despite the differences in their appearances, it was found that they interbreed freely in the Great Plains of Central USA and most birds are hybrids known as The Northern Oriole…

Hybrids…? Do you mean mongrels?

"…Icterus galbula."

Bingo! Mongrel!

The band of birdwatchers nodded approvingly, but Ben ignored them. There was much more he was not telling them about this family of birds, about the reclusive Black-headed Oriole furtively skirting the Mexican Border or the insectivorous Hooded Oriole ignoring the duty of the genus to re-seed through their excretions. For the moment….in fact for many moments since he had given things any thought, these birds, like the pretender Lichtenstein's Oriole, seemed beside the point. The point was the fictional "Baltimore" Oriole, the bird with the quotes around its name in every textbook and field guide in North America. And, the point was beyond his science; it was beyond the affirming gravity of his data. Like a small feather floating in the air, the bird's true identity had suddenly eluded Ben's grasp.

Feeling himself to be deep in some primordial forest, he continued on…obscuring things.

"Actually, I was born in Baltimore…and, I must say, I was an Oriole fan myself. I mean a fan of the baseball team. It was a real disappointment to learn that the bird, ha hah…was not as real as everyone thought." Ben looked up at the sky; he did not want to meet the gaze of the birdwatchers.

Actually…it changed the world as you knew it! This fictitious bird held a solid position within popular understanding of birdlife. It was nestled right in there with the Robins and Sparrows, a little prettier perhaps but as reliable as the rest. Even when the clever interloper's fiction was uncovered it was too late. No one wanted to let it go. Calling the bird a "Northern" Oriole was like calling a Red-winged Blackbird a Blackbird with red wings. It was like recruiting an entirely new team. It was changing the very chemistry of the thing. The Baltimore Oriole was specific. It meant something! The "Northern" Oriole isn't even acceptable as an expansion team. North is no place… it's just a general area, an arbitrary celestial direction.

Ben continued, "I seem to recall finding out about this while reading *Life Magazine*. You probably don't remember the original Life Magazine; it had a very good science section….ha hah."

Another child's underpinnings knocked apart by an innocent intrusion into the magazine rack. Where is that weird chuckle coming from?

"Anyway," Ben said, wibbling further off point, "You're better off rooting for the St. Louis Cardinals; then, at least, you know what you're rooting for…a baseball team and not a bird."

By now, the group had begun to move on, their heads both nodding and swiveling in the manner that heads do when their owners are expressing understanding and disinterest at the same time. They were not really interested in baseball teams. They were interested in *real* birds and their heads swiveled like radar dishes hoping to intercept a flight path, any flight path.

Ben lagged behind. Still grinning with half his face, he cocked his head sideways and punched his fist into his palm. Things were becoming clearer. As a grown rational man of science, Ben had occasionally experienced a mild and not unpleasant synaptic disruption due to the overlapping of the Baltimore Oriole as *both* ornithoid-being and baseball cap symbol; however, the circuit was now fully blown. Rotating about himself, he realized that in some peculiar way, he had always believed the bird to have been named after the baseball team and not the other way around…or, at least, they had shared the name for the same reason.

He remembered 1954. He was only five years old when The St. Louis Browns baseball team was bought by a group of baseball men from Washington, D.C. There was already a team in Washington, so the Browns were installed 30 miles away in downtown Baltimore's Memorial Stadium and re-named the Baltimore Orioles. Vice-President Richard Nixon threw out the first ball and the peculiar Oriole fan was born.

It is said that Oriole fans are unique to baseball, a happy blend of southern propriety and northern presumption, the only fans that appear both deeply apologetic and apoplectic when booing their opponents. But like the city itself, Baltimoreans also seem to have unto themselves an air of contented dislocation. They are, in fact, neither northerners nor southerners, known best by their easternness and centeredness, as in…the "mid-Atlantic states."

Ben spent much of 1954 at Memorial Stadium in the care of an irreverent row-house widow named Thelma Bishop. "Bishie", as she was known, was Ben's babysitter; the Stadium was her daycare center. An avid Oriole fan and holder of loud opinions on the national pastime, Bishie believed that baseball provided a fine synthesis of all that was good in the world, and all that could go bad if someone, namely herself, was not paying careful attention. She considered herself a master statistician and strategist, quick to tell Ben what the pitcher should throw next, where a fielder should align himself, on which side of the runner the batter should drive the ball, and so on. She conveyed these directives to Ben with her head turned down to him but her eyes on the field as if it was understood that he was to pass this information directly on to the eagerly awaiting Oriole dugout. Indeed, Ben's earliest memory of these days was his embarrassment for the player who had somehow missed the relayed signals.

The days with "The Orioles" came to an abrupt close when Ben's family moved out of state, leaving the team to prosper as the winningest team in baseball for the next thirty years. It also so happened that these thirty years were the only ones remaining in Bishie's life. She had appreciated baseball, but she had *loved* that baseball team—there was a difference; this was her lesson and Ben's inheritance. Although he could never quite explain why, Ben had come to feel the same. Deeply.

He had not thought much about Bishie after joining the sanctuary but now, here in this scrub forest, she had alighted on his shoulder, an overdue memory admonishing him with a wink and an elbow in the ribs. She had been the namer of things for the young boy – an Ann Sullivan to Ben's Helen Keller, placing the object in one hand while spelling the word that named it in the other. The difference was that Bishie had given him two things with the same name and he had gone forward into the world, slightly askew, smiling goofily, like a kid showing off his new shoes on the wrong feet.

As a boy, he had simply and with the utmost understanding assumed the bird and the baseball team to have been named for the same reason (somewhat like… ah ha, *over there* is an unusual bird with qualities a, b, and c. I shall name it "X". And look, *over there*… a fine young bunch of baseball players. They too have qualities a, b, and c and although these are baseball qualities and not bird qualities, it doesn't really matter since I admire them both in the same sort of way. As such, I shall also name this team of fine young baseball players: "X"). It was fine for them both to be named "X" because "X" was what was important and which had meaning. Not an accepted meaning nor, in most circles, even an acceptable meaning; however, it was meaning enough for a child to take a few timid steps forward into the world and that was precisely what Ben did. Later, as a young man turning to science, he had begun to stumble.

Ignoring a vague discomfort, the young man of science established a new sense of order with this shape-shifting name (*of course, the bird, Icterus galbula, has nothing whatsoever to do with the baseball team; that would be as preposterous as believing the San Francisco Giants to be a yahooing, tobacco-chewing, rump-slapping band of Gullivers jogging ashore to play baseball for the Bay Area Lilliputians, ha ha ha*) and, having dispensed with that problem, continued about his business. Then, one day, the bird's name itself was canceled by some ornithological stock room clerks rearranging scientific inventory and, when this taxonomic change occurred, he had done a peculiar thing: he had pretended not to notice.

And now, drifting farther and farther behind the birdwatchers, connected to them like a forgotten balloon bobbing reluctantly at the end of a long string, Ben did take notice. He realized that at the moment the fiction quotes embraced that bird's name, its very life had been sucked out it and along with it had gone a big piece of Ben's childhood. The boy, father to the man, had been orphaned.

Ben stopped and welcomed Bishie; she had come back to babysit.

They were out of the forest now and the birdwatchers were standing expectantly before the gift shop. Fumbling in his pockets, Ben realized that he had lost his key somewhere along the trail. Only slightly disappointed, the birdwatchers mumbled their thanks and returned to their cars, happy enough to be rid of the dotty pre-occupied fellow and the few disappointing crows still flying overhead.

Ben dutifully watched them leave and then, still gripping tightly to his binoculars, turned back into the sanctuary and began to retrace his steps, barely resisting the urge to run.

Author's Endnote: For much of the 20th century, popular culture had always used the designation "Baltimore" for the Oriole, but the scientific community used "Northern." Genetic tests have restored the bird to its proper place both in the world and in popular imagination.

"Meet the" Vignettes
Peter Matthiessen Wheelwright

Who are you?

You'd probably be better off asking others who I *am*. Like everyone else, I'd just make up a story.

That said, here's what I *do*: I was trained as an architect, practiced and taught design in New York City at Parsons School of Design where I live (when not birdwatching in rural upstate New York), and began writing literary fiction when I tired of my first two occupations.

What was the inspiration for your piece?

As for "The Life of Birds," I was inspired to conflate my affection for the natural world with my love for my favorite baseball team, the Baltimore Orioles. Much of the story is, in fact, factual...which is to say autobiographical. I do indeed go back to 1954 (...you can now do the math to know how old I am), and I was there. With her.

Who's your favorite player?

Diamond Jim Gentile the Orioles first baseman was my hero, and one day I will write a story about my grumpiness over his misfortune of having his 1961 MVP year at the same time Mickey Mantle was chasing and Roger Maris overtook Babe Ruth's home run record. Coming in third as MVP behind those guys still renders him and his accomplishments invisible. At least my favorite memory, his consecutive grand slams against Pedro Ramos and Paul Giel of the Twins in May of that year, still has total recall in the announcers' booths.

What's the highlight of your writing career?

I suppose the highlight of my writing career is a toss-up between a PEN/Hemingway Honorable Mention for my first novel, *As It Is On Earth*, and a "Best Books of 2022" from *The New Yorker* for the second, *The Door-Man*.

Favorite baseball book?

My favorite book to this day is *Baseball Bonus Kid* which was given to me for Xmas in 1961 and set me on course to actually *become* a Baltimore Oriole.

Sadly, it didn't work out.

Q: Which prize did Peter Matthiessen Wheelwright win from *The Twin Bill*?
A: 2023 Jackie Mitchell Creative Nonfiction Prize

Illustration by Sam Williams

Duck
By Scott Bolohan

HIS REAL NAME WASN'T DUCK, of course.

But Shane Thompson was born syndactyly, causing skin to connect his ring and pinky fingers up to just below the knuckle. The condition occurs to about one in 2,500, but it wasn't completely unexpected, as his grandfather was as well. But the webbing was deemed simply cosmetic and wouldn't interfere with the functionality of his hands. His parents, soon to be divorced and barely getting by as it was, weren't interested in any extra expenses.

Shane had a relatively normal childhood with his grandfather in rural Pennsylvania. It wasn't until the great American tradition of the handprint turkey art around Thanksgiving that Shane realized there was something different about him. Perhaps it was indifference or childhood innocence, but it took years for anyone else to notice.

It started with quacks behind his back. And then when he played tag in gym, one of the girls screamed when he tagged her.

He was Duck now, irreversibly.

His teacher told the class not to call people names, which just made everything worse. So he tried to pretend he didn't hear anything the kids said and stopped doing anything that would draw attention to his hands. At recess, he read books.

The night before his first day of fourth grade, his grandfather found Shane in his room crying. "I was wondering when this would happen, happened to me too," he said, holding up his hands. "Nothing to be ashamed of. Ducks are some of the most intelligent animals, quick learners. You know what I did that made those kids furious? I embraced it. I still have friends who call me Duck."

The next day at class, Shane asked his teacher if she would call him Duck. After a great deal of hesitancy, and the insistence from his grandfather that it was okay, he was officially Duck.

At recess, he started playing sports again. If they were playing football, he was playing quarterback. If he was playing baseball, he was on the mound.

When he was 12, his grandpa taught him a circle changeup, tucking his thumb under his index fingers, the ring finger against the seam, the webbing between his ring finger and pinky neatly wrapping against the ball. The first time he threw it in a game, the batter was so far ahead of it that, yes, Duck snorted.

***

Scouting Report			OFP		**3**
Name:	Shane Thompson				
Date:	5/15/22				
Team:	Susquehanna University				
Organization:					
Age	22		DOB	4/13/2000	
Position:	SP		B/T	L/L	

Size

Height:	5'10"		Weight	180	
Observations:	Undersized. Not much growth potential.				

Delivery			Grade	4	5
Smooth	Herky	Upright	Athletic	~~Rushed~~	~~Slow~~
From Stretch					
Command	Hits Spots	~~Behind~~	Ahead	Control	Command
Arm Speed	Quick	~~Rushed~~	Long	~~Short~~	
Description	Low 3/4 with deception. Hides ball well. More athletic than appears.				
Results	Plus control with a real feel for pitching.				

FB			Grade	2	25
Velocity	Sit	Low	High		
	83	79	85		
Description:	Well located with lots of tail.				
Results	Weak contact on the ground and even a few swings and misses.				

Breaking Ball			Grade	4	4
Velocity	Sit	Low	High	Type	
	70	68	71	12-6	
Description:	Sharp, classic 12-6 action, didn't have great feel for the pitch.				
Results	Used mostly against lefties, produced poor swings.				

Changeup/BB 2			Grade	7	8
Velocity	Sit	Low	High	Type	
	72	67	74	Circle Change	
Description:	I do not say this lightly, this may be the best changeup I've ever seen. Incredible armside action.				
Results	Fooled every hitter. Sometimes bounced before the plate and get swings. No solid contact. Truly elite pitch.				

***

Ducks Pitcher Giving Fans Something to Quack About

CENTRAL ISLIP, N.Y.

Fans are hoping this is the start of a 'Duck dynasty.'

Since joining the Ducks, Shane "Duck" Thompson has thrown twenty-six consecutive scoreless innings. The secret? His devastating changeup.

"My grandpa taught it to me when I was young," Thompson said. "I was real self-conscious of my hands, but finding baseball gave me something I could be proud of."

What may seem like a publicity stunt—a guy nicknamed Duck playing for the Long Island Ducks—couldn't be further from the truth. Thompson has dominated this year and won over the hearts of Ducks fans.

I've never seen the fans embrace anyone like Duck before.

The Ducks leaned into the nickname, playing "Rubber Duckie" from *Sesame Street* for his intro music, encouraging the fans to chant 'quack' by playing *Mighty Ducks* clips, and even holding a rubber duck giveaway night, which didn't quite go according to plan.

After Thompson picked up the final out, the fans threw their rubber ducks on the field, turning the field into a sea of yellow.

"That was pretty crazy," Thompson said. "Obviously I'm glad they didn't do it when the game was still going on and that no one got hurt. I'll always remember it, but I don't think they'll have another one of those nights again."

The team confirmed Thompson was right.

Thompson said he started going by Duck when he was a kid but had never been called 'Rubber Duck' before since he was mostly a starting pitcher. Now that he pitches in nearly every game, he said it makes sense.

"It's fun, I like it," Thompson said of the nickname. "I've been called worse things."

The Ducks sit in first place and are attracting attention on social media. Videos of Thompson's intro and the fans quacking and blowing duck whistles—which were subsequently banned by the league after complaints of the incessant noise—have been shared nearly a million times. Not bad for a team with around 15,000 followers on Twitter.

"Duck has breathed new light into this organization and the league," Ducks GM Stephen Ramsey said. "He's been great to work with, whenever we have an idea for a video, he's always game."

Thompson credits his grandfather for showing him his changeup. He was able to attend Rubber Duck night, the first time he saw Duck play professional ball. At the end of the game, he tossed his grandfather the ball from the final out.

"He was pretty emotional," Thompson said. "To hear the crowd chant for me like they did, it always means a lot to me, but it meant even more to him."

Thompson's nickname comes from the webbing between his pinky and ring fingers caused by syndactyly. He doesn't know if it helps his famous changeup, but he says it "couldn't hurt."

Thompson was a Division III second-team All-American last season as a starting pitcher at Susquehanna University but went undrafted before signing with the Long Island Ducks as bullpen help. He hopes to become the third player from his alma mater, and the first since Bob Clark pitched for Cleveland in 1921, to make the major leagues.

"I've been facing an uphill battle my whole life," Thompson said. "It's been my dream to make it to the big leagues ever since I first picked up a baseball. It honestly changed my life, gave me something I knew I was good at and could be proud of. I'm going to take this as far as I can go."

***

September 14, 2028

Gramps,

You'll never guess where I'm writing this. I'm on a plane to New York. I got called up to the big leagues. I wasn't sure this would ever happen, and trust me, I know I wasn't the only one. But you always believed in me. When I was told I didn't throw hard enough for college, I was too small to go pro, all those years barely making any money in indy ball and the minors, every time I had someone tell me I couldn't do something, I thought about you and knew I could.

These last couple years have been hard. There were so many times I thought about quitting. I wish you could be here with me tonight. I know you'll never get to read this letter, but I'm going to keep it in my pocket during my games. It'll be like you're still here with me.

Love,

Duck

***

"After spending four years in the independent leagues and climbing his way up through the minor league system, Shane "Duck" Thompson is making his major league debut. This kid has quite a story. They call him Duck because his fingers are webbed. He only tops out in the mid-80s, but he's supposed to have one impressive changeup."

"Ask any major leaguer what the hardest pitch to hit is, and you know what they'll tell you? It's a changeup."

"His debut comes at a tough spot, two on, two out in the 10th. Martinez is the hitter, one-for-four on the day with a single. He's struggled against lefties this year. Fastball on the outside part of the plate for strike one."

"That was only 83, almost like it was too slow for Martinez."

"Thompson, 28, was a member of the Long Island Ducks for three years, winning two championships with them not too far from here. Now he's making his debut at Yankee Stadium in front of a sold-out crowd. Thompson kicks and here's the pitch. Strike two, slow curve ball on the inner half of the plate."

"I don't think Martinez was expecting that. Everyone in the ballpark was thinking changeup."

"You'd have to think he'll go to it now. Duck checks the runners. Here's the pitch. Swung on and hit in the air, back goes Anderson. It is high, it is far, it is gone! Martinez walks it off! Ballgame Over! Yankees win! Thaaaaa Yankees win!"

***

TRANSACTIONS September 16, 2028

Major League Baseball

American League

BOSTON RED SOX — Designated OF Eduardo Rojas for assignment. Claimed SS Aiden Ward off waivers from Tampa Bay.

NEW YORK YANKEES —Sent INF Wil Valdez outright to Scranton/Wilkes-Barre (IL). Optioned C Ben Barnabas to Scranton/Wilkes-Barre.

TAMPA BAY RAYS — Transferred LHP Felix Miranda from the 15-day IL to the 60-day IL. Placed LHP Jerome Malone on the restricted list. Selected the contracts of LHPs Cooper Chadwick, Javy Bautista and RHP Joaquin Alfonso from Durham (IL). Optioned RHP Emerson Michaels and LHP Shane Thompson to Durham.

TEXAS RANGERS — Recalled RHP Erick Aguayo from Round Rock (PCL).

National League

MIAMI MARLINS — Optioned LHP Andrew Nichols to Jacksonville (IL). Selected the contract of RHP Bryan Zorn from Jacksonville. Recalled RHP Kyle Haring from Jacksonville.

PITTSBURGH PIRATES — Recalled INF Franklyn Castillo from Indianapolis (IL). Optioned INF Harold Park to Indianapolis.

Q: Scott Bolohan played on the same high school baseball team as what major leaguer?

A: Jon Berti

Illustration by Jason David Córdova

Set Position
By Shea West

By Shea West

DON'T FORGET TO BREATHE.

This is the one rule your father never gave you, but it's the one that you use throughout all of the strikeouts in your life. The way that you settle into the rhythm of your breathing is part routine, part superstition, in the same way that Marino rubs his lucky rabbit's foot before taking first base and the way that Johnson never shaves his mustache for the entire season.

Place your pivot foot against the pitching rubber.

Historically it's been easy for men to use sports analogies to explain things to their sons, and so your father issues the twelve baseball rules to help you through the infields and outfields of your childhood. Twelve feels like so many rules at once, yet it takes twelve months for your mother and father to be ruled out on the double play. Your mother and father are two offensive players on the same team. The officials call this a "pitcher's best friend," but you don't think there is anything friendly about the way your parents continue to field ground balls at one another.

Face both shoulders to first base because you're a lefty.

He makes sure to invite you to the table of manhood one sweltering summer day, thirty miles away in his new home. Thirty miles or a 45-minute drive. That's how far away your father moved when he and your mother ended things. You've always been a numbers guy. 91.7 mph fastball with 2.0 IP, 0 H, 0 R, 0 ER, 0 BB, 3 K, 0 HR, 29-18 PC-ST, 2.58 ERA.

But sometimes your shoulders face third because you're ambidextrous.

The thing about sitting at the table is–as a boy you know that acting self-important is frowned upon– but as a man, you can act however you want. As an adult, your father doesn't have to build the table— his arrogance is enough to sit there feeling chesty and unaccountable for his actions. Accepting the invite feels like a switch hit driven into your mother's heart, but you want to hear your father out. And so you sit at the table anyway.

Hold the ball in both hands in front of you.

Your father chooses that day to toss you a baseball, much like the one that's in your hands right now. It's a brand-new ball, one without any scuffs and white leather that shines so bright you hesitate to hold the damn thing. Preservation of the ball in this moment feels necessary and so you cradle it in your hands and pray that your palms don't sweat and cause the red dye of the threading to bleed. Bleeding is hard to stop.

This is your set position.

Your father says to you, "Son, it's time you learned how to play the game."

This is a milestone that signifies you've arrived at the doors of manhood, even if your voice hasn't dropped to a rich baritone just yet. Other boys in the neighborhood receive baseballs from their dads, while you know that this is symbolic, you never expect your father to give you one. You find it funny that your father waits until he moves 45 minutes away to finally show you some sort of attention.

Bring the ball up to your chest.

The ball in your hands is an invite that you aren't expecting—one that says you can be on the same team with your father. You do your best to not act outwardly surprised, but your insides turn like Marino when his feet pound from first, to second, to third. The bottom half of your still chubby, undefined chin hangs open as if you'd just witnessed The Great Bambino himself hit a home run.

Force the runner back to first with a false step.

Your father asks why you look green in the gills, and you just shrug because fewer words with your old man is always easier. He isn't good at coaching you about how to act around girls or how to get the perfect shave. You think it impossible that this man can teach you about the dynamics of ball throwing. Pitching and throwing are precise, and precision is something your father fails at in every aspect.

Return to set position, wait for the signal from your catcher.

You search your brain for another time when your father looks as serious as he does now, and you come up with nothing. He's always been an easy-going guy, never one to get his feathers ruffled or to cry foul when the universe slights him. Head nods and nose swipes are all decoy signs that he wants to be a dad and not to execute the play of being a family man. He wants to steal home plate and speed up the whole game of life, and revel in the celebration that comes with scoring a run.

Two fingers point down and swirl to the right, you nod your head in agreement.

The smell of his aftershave is stronger than usual, a mix of sage and spiced cloves decorate the air. The aroma announces that this day will remain a part of your sense memory, in the way that the dirt on the ball field after a heavy summer rain does now. Your father goes to great strides to demonstrate that this is a special day.

"We're going down to the field," he says.

That's all he mutters, but it is enough to feel caught in a pickle between him and your mother.

It's a blind pickoff, but you trust your catcher.

The field by your father's home is much greener than the one by your mother's house. There are field lights and a covered shelter over the benches, with a perfectly sloped pitcher's mound. The field is unaffected by players with coarse-bottomed cleats, the kind that can destroy the green and rip into your skin when colliding with the third baseman. He rattles off the rules before he even shows you how to hold the ball.

"Never give up. It's okay to strike out. Do your absolute best. Teamwork is the best work." You stop him at that rule, as your father is a poor teammate if there ever was one.

Drive the ball to the second baseman.

Before you become a pitcher yourself, you consider becoming an umpire for a bit. You think if you can control the play on the field and bench players for unsportsmanlike conduct everything will be copasetic.

"Whose team are you on, dad?"

Watch the showdown between the first and second baseman with your glove open.

He ignores the slight and continues with more rules.

"Keep your eye on the ball." He holds the ball right in front of you for emphasis.

"Aim for the fences. Always swing hard. Cheaters never win."

Well, that was rich, you thought.

Scoop up the loose ball and tag the player out. Caught trying to steal.

The mound you stand on makes you feel ten feet tall. You, in this moment, are a bigger man than he will ever be. You haven't played the field yet, and you know immediately to put pressure on your old man and pitch hard. The small expanse of your chest barrels into him and you both fall from the mound into the dirt.

Set your position, no wild pitches.

He lays there as if he's been waiting for you to pummel him. He wants a punishment in the form of a split lip to brandish like a pennant for the world series of fatherhood. You stand back up in shock at your explosion. Your father wipes the blood from his lip and stares at the smear on the back of his hand. Bleeding is hard to stop and your father continues on with his ridiculous rules anyway.

"Sacrifice yourself in the most crucial of moments. Your brain is your most important muscle."

Face the batter. Wind up. Breathe.

As you make your way back to the mound, you let your bloodied father stare at your back for longer than you know he feels comfortable. The heart has always been your most important muscle. The thing that pumps blood through your entire circulatory system. The heart muscle gives your brain oxygen, and without it, there'd be no way for your brain to be capable of sustaining the kind of heartbreak your father creates in your world.

Your back is still turned when your father mutters through a soft sob. "If it's what you love, never stop loving."

Follow through on the pitch and strike the batter out.

You think back on that day when your father dirtied himself in his field errors, bloodied and brazen enough to bestow rules upon you. He is not the kind of man that you will look up to for advice on your knuckleball or your changeup.

He is not your coach. Hell, he's not much of a father.

Your body remains hunched over the mound from the follow-through as you watch the batter swing and strike out. If you abide by any of the "rules" your father gave you, it's the last one. You kiss the leather of your dusty glove and point to the stands and smile at your mother. Watch her smile with pride as she wipes small tears from her eyes and you know that this display of affection is not a decoy signal. You answer the call from your mother as you cross home plate and meet your catcher and realize that you only need two rules to make it through this life.

Don't forget to breathe and return to a set position.

ANGELS

Illustration by Mark Mosley

Major League Dad
By Jack Smiles

I LOOKED AT HIS ENTRY in my Macmillan Baseball Encyclopedia so many times it flips opens to page 1006 at a touch. His entry says he was 5'11" and 180 lbs. Says his name was Frank Krischeck and his nickname was "Bulldog." Says he batted left and threw left; was born in 1937 in Kanock, PA; played seven seasons in the majors with two different teams from 1962 to 1968. What Macmillan doesn't say is Frank Krischeck is my dad.

* * *

In 1956, Dad was drafted by Cleveland out of Kanock High, where he'd been an all-state running back as well as a pitcher with an assortment of pitches, including one of his own invention: the knuckle drop. With stops at Selma, Alabama, and Minot, North Dakota, it took him until '60 to work his way up to AAA Salt Lake, where the air must have been too salty or too dry, because the knuckle didn't drop and Dad got hammered all over the yard. When he got passed over in the Indians September call-up, they released him. It looked like the end. Expansion saved him. The expansion LA Angels chose him in the special player draft in October of '61.

The Angels kept my dad down at AAA to start the '62 season, if you can call Hawaii a downer. That September it finally happened: my dad, Frank Krischeck, became a major league ballplayer while getting a sip of coffee in the September call-up. He got in one game. He pitched to seven batters and didn't get any of them out. Four of them scored and left Dad with an ERA of infinity for '61. It's right there in Macmillan, that squiggly symbol in the ERA column.

By 1962, Dad was 27 and back to Hawaii. Figuring pitching ball in paradise was better than working, Dad wouldn't give it up.

As he stepped off the plane in Hawaii in March '63, he met a waitress at the Hula Grill Waikiki. Her name was Lana and she put a lei around his neck. By mid-July, after a couple of Angels went down with arm problems, my father went back to California. This time he stuck, and he never came back.

In 1964 for the Angels, Dad mopped up a 14–2 loss to the Yankees in Yankee Stadium and gave up Mantle's 410th home run. I got the chills when I learned that.

The Angels released him in July. Over the winter he signed with the Phillies, but he couldn't get anybody out and the Phillies released him in May. He was two months shy of his 31st birthday. There were no takers. He was done. That's when he moved in with his mother at the old homestead on Hill Street in Kanock, PA.

He walked into her kitchen, grabbed a beer, and sat down at the kitchen table. She looked at him and said, "Now what?"

His old high school teammate, Bill Bohn, owned a Bud distributorship. He gave Dad a job selling a product that sold itself in an area with more liquor licenses per capita than Vegas. Bohn figured all Dad had to do was walk into an establishment and the proprietors would throw money at him, agog at their one and only bona fide homegrown major leaguer.

I learned most of this stuff about my dad long after the fact from my Uncle Russ, my dad's brother.

* * *

My mom was only 19 and didn't even know she was pregnant until after Dad left Hawaii for LA in July of '63. I was born the following February. She named me Shane and gave me her last name. She never tried to contact my father, figuring he wouldn't make much of a dad. When I was 12, Mom told me the truth about Dad.

"He was a no-account ballplayer who took advantage of a teenager. It was a one-night stand and he never called again."

A ballplayer? I told my Little League teammates about it. They either rolled their eyes or laughed. I saved up $19.95 delivering papers and bought a first edition Macmillan and wore it out looking at my dad's entry and studying every team he played on. A sportswriter at the Honolulu Advertiser who knew him told me stories about the partying. He laughed like crazy. The writer arranged access to the Advertiser's morgue and I photocopied box scores and game stories of his appearances with the Islanders, but I couldn't find a picture. There were team pictures, but on the microfilm I couldn't make out his face. I looked for baseball cards, but nobody in Hawaii, at least that I could find, saved nine-year-old baseball cards of obscure pitchers.

Through a pen pal program at my school I exchanged letters with a kid my age in California by the name of Rex. He found two Frank Krischeck baseball cards and sent them to me. When I looked at his rookie card I thought I was looking in a mirror. I showed them to my teammates and they said, "Holy crap."

After I graduated from high school, I decided to look for Frank Krischeck.

* * *

Rex's parents were nice: they put me in the efficiency above their garage. From there, I wrote letters to Major League Baseball, the Angels, and the Phillies, asking for the last known address of Frank Krischeck. Not one wrote back. Telephone Information in Pennsylvania had a Krischeck. They said they had heard of Frank, the former ballplayer, but didn't know if he was still in town.

Rex's parents were flea marketers and on Sunday mornings they took Rex and me along. Rex and I browsed books and baseball cards. One day I stumbled on a thin paperback and couldn't believe my eyes when I looked at the cover of "Addresses of Former Major League Baseball Players." I'd never known such a book existed, but there it was in my hands for 10 cents. And there on page 32 was Frank Krischeck, 111 Hill Street, Kanock, PA. The book was seven years old.

Rex wanted me to call and warn my dad before I just walked in on him and introduced myself as the son he never knew he had, but we couldn't get a number. It was just as well. I didn't want to call, didn't want to give him a chance to deny or reject me from 3,000 miles away.

That night I stuffed a change of underwear, a couple pairs of jeans, and two T-shirts in my backpack around my Macmillan. The next morning I walked to the Greyhound station and bought a ticket for Harrisburg, PA—which, the ticket agent said, was as close as he could get me to Kanock. It was a three-day ride to Pennsylvania and along the way I studied an atlas and a Pennsylvania guidebook I had bought at a flea market.

Kanock was up in the mountains. Half the county was a National Forest and the other half was game lands. There were tons of streams and lakes. Sounded like a place that might have more deer than people.

* * *

I got there mid-afternoon. 111 Hill Street, Kanock, PA. It looked like an old farmhouse. With rookie butterflies, I knocked on the door. A woman with grey hair answered. She asked me what did I want and then said, "Ohmigod," as she peered at my face. "You're the spittin' image of…"

She didn't finish her sentence, but I got the meaning. Turned out Dad was gone overnight on a sales trip to Erie, so she called my uncle Russ who came right over. A letter written by my mom explained everything.

Russ sat me down and filled in the blanks in Dad's story. We talked for hours. When I went on and on about how excited and proud I was to have a Major League Dad, Uncle Russ gave me a warning. He

146

said Dad was embarrassed about his baseball career and his lifestyle back then. Said Dad carried on as if it never happened and he likely wouldn't talk about it. He even made my grandma, Helen, delist the phone number.

"He was the best and proudest athlete ever to come out of Kanock," Russ said. "So, what do they talk about? He gave up Mantle's 410th home run—a 500-foot job. Once hit three batters in a row to force in a run and lose a game. Never reached the postseason. Finished with a losing record for a bunch of lousy teams. And there's that infinity thing. He's embarrassed, too, about the partying and the fooling around."

Russ explained that Dad was a little bitter about the money, too. His highest Major League salary was $17,500, total for the nine seasons was $60,000. He'd only been out of the game six years when his old Phillies teammate Dick Allen signed a quarter-million-dollar contract with the White Sox.

After Russ left, my new grandma sent me to the shower and told me I could wait up for Dad on the couch. But after I fell asleep in front of a Phillies game, she sent me to bed in a spare bedroom, which used to be Uncle Russ's. After three days and nights on buses, I slept.

When I opened my eyes, a man was sitting at the foot of the bed. He was old and gray-haired. My father, the Frank Krischeck I knew from baseball cards, was barely older than I was. Time had stopped for me when it came to my father—stopped in 1961, with him 25 years old, on the mound in the major leagues. Stopped with him smiling back at me from a baseball card.

***

Shakey's was one of the many bars in and around Kanock where sports fans hung out. No matter what time it was, it may as well have been midnight. The small portal windows were curtained. There were six guys sitting at the bar under a haze of blue smoke. Before Shakey could say a thing, my dad blurted out, "If you still want me to sign that old uniform for the back bar, it's okay."

Shakey raised an eyebrow and went in the back to get the uniform. One of the guys at the bar blew a smoke ring and asked, "Does that mean you're finally going to tell us if that infinity thing stood for the number of Annies you met?"

They all hooted and laughed.

"Yeah," said another one of the guys, "and what about the homer you gave up to Mantle, I heard it's still going?" More laughter.

"Let me tell you about that," Dad said. He leaned in close to the bar and the guys gathered around. "I never told anybody this before," he said barely above a whisper. "I grooved him one because he promised he'd take me to the Copacabana that night."

They all screamed with laughter, jumping from their stools or burying their heads in their folded arms on the bar.

"Hey Shakey," one of them yelled, "pour old Bulldog here a shot and a beer."

Q: What prize did this short story win?

A: 2023 Sidd Finch Fiction Prize

Illustration by Andy Lattimer

Last Night at 498
By Kyle Bilinski

JOHNNY "NONSTOP" MILES COULDN'T SLEEP on game nights. He listened to the static baby monitor linked up to his boys across the hall and thought about the pitchers he'd soon face—their heaters, their junk, the ticks of their windups. His wife turned and curled against him again, kicked a leg over his shin, and breathed into his shoulder. Her soft puffs reminded him of the way he tried to steady his lungs in the batter's box, hungry for something fat, aching to connect. That's when he heard a click and creak downstairs. His wife didn't stir, but he slid out from under the bedsheets and fumbled for his Louisville Slugger under the bedframe and rushed into the hall for the three-way switch.

It felt like waiting for smoke to dissipate or fog to clear, waiting for his eyes to adjust to the bright can lights overhead. Then he appeared on the landing below, tall but fragile looking, with a nylon stocking and SF cap pulled down over his head, a belly gun in his grip.

"Rings, diamonds, pearls, cash," he said.

"My wife called 911," Johnny said, which was a good lie. "You have two, maybe three minutes before the cops show up," he added, then explained how close the nearest police station was to his unassuming two-story in the Outer Sunset, which overlooked the Great Highway and Ocean Beach.

The stocking distorted his face, smashing his nose and cheeks, and the hat bill shadowed his eyes. "Rings, diamonds, pearls, now," he said and waved the gun behind Johnny.

"My bambinos are dreaming," Johnny said and took a slow step down. "You can have anything you want downstairs, on your way out. You're not coming upstairs." He took another step but halted when he saw the perfect circle of the barrel.

"Jewelry," the man shouted.

"Don't you know we're on the same team?" Johnny said and pointed at the man's cap. "I'm Nonstop Miles, your big slugger." He took another slow step. "We're on the same team, man."

They moved like opposite poled magnets, repelling one another. The man backed down the steps towards the front door with a hand on the railing and the other on the gun, and Johnny rested the bat against his shoulder as if he were waiting for a pitch, gripping it two-handed as he pushed the man away from his family. But staring at the barrel of the snub-nosed revolver made him feel like he was 15 again—the last time he remembered feeling so timid and afraid—when his junior varsity coach asked him stay late one night after practice to stand on the inside line of the batter's box with 50-pound sandbags straddling his spiked cleats, anchoring him to the dirt. His coach took to the rubber with a five-gallon bucket of balls and hurled two-seamed zingers in at his wrists, up at his temple, back at his shoulder blades, and made him twist out of the way or take the blows to his body, one bruiser after the other, to get over his crippling fear of getting hit by the pitch.

"The car keys are on the hook," Johnny said. "Take them if you want."

The man reached for the doorknob but not the keys. Sirens sounded in the near distance, which meant that Clara had woken up, that she'd seen the light and heard their voices, and made the call. He knew that she'd have crossed the hall by now, pressed her back up against the door to Frank's and Hank's room, and was praying to God to protect them all.

"Take it," Johnny said and offered up the knob of his bat. "It's signed by The Big Hurt, from his '97 season." THOMAS was etched in big block letters with a Sharpie signature below, from a game his mom had taken him to at Comiskey—a couple miles from where he'd been born and raised by her alone. He could sense the man's fear and desperation, his sudden immobility, now that they were close. "It's worth a small fortune," Johnny said. "Take it, now." He shoved the two-toned barrel into the man's grip and gut, pushing him outside in the darkness before blue and red lights swirled down the street.

Johnny hated sirens, flashing lights. He'd seen enough of those to last a lifetime in South Chicago before he'd signed with the Giants and come west. Even after the officers left, after they'd searched the gridwork of neighboring streets and written a report, he couldn't shake them out of his brain. Clara helped him pull their sofa across their family room and pin it up against the front door. They triple-checked deadbolts and window latches before hiking upstairs to look in on the boys. Johnny hovered over their cribs, got within inches of Frank's and Hank's lips to hear their breathing. Their sound machine and thick curtains had kept them insulated, unaware.

Johnny turned up the static of the monitor once they crashed back in bed, which helped him calm down. But Clara needed to talk, needed to process. She set her head on his chest and told him how panicked she'd been that he'd get shot and that she wouldn't be able to protect the boys afterward. "Shhh," he told her, not to stop her from talking but to soothe her. "Shhh," he said again and rubbed her back. It was the same thing he'd learned to do with Frank and Hank when they were upset in the middle of the night. They regularly woke up together and he'd ball them up against his chest and neck and rub their tiny backs and butts. "Shhh," he'd say over and over, like he was doing now with Clara, until they settled.

Johnny rested his eyes but never fell back to sleep; his brain never stopped. He thought about calling security companies to wire an alarm. He thought about adding a hotel-style chain lock himself in the meantime. Then, eventually, images of windups and release points and two-seemed fastballs overtook memories of the man's smashed face and belly gun. And he thought about how incredibly close he was to joining the 500-homerun club—just two more four-baggers and he'd become 29th on the list—and how much he wanted to do this at home in San Francisco, in front of his family and the only fans he'd known outside of his childhood in Chicago. He ran through all his idols on the list—Hammerin' Hank, The Say Hey Kid, Mr. October, The Big Hurt himself, and The Thomenator—but tried to push the extra pressures and nervousness out of mind until the boys got him up around six-thirty in the morning.

The next few hours rushed by. He always let Clara sleep late on mornings when he was home, and now that the boys were starting to crawl, keeping them corralled and away from the stairs wasn't easy. He liked feeding them most—a baby in either arm with warmed milk bottles to start, followed by scrambled eggs, cereal puffs, and apple sauce in their highchairs. Then they were all back on the floor, pulling books from shelves, toys from baskets, until Clara found them and told Johnny he'd better shower and hop on the train.

The N Judah metro line platform stood four blocks from his house. Johnny took his time walking since he couldn't see a train parked. He was still warm from his shower, but the foggy ocean air cooled him down. He'd started dressing down on his commute to the park—sneakers, sweatpants, hoodie, and cap; everything solid black with orange stitching and discreet detailing—rather than wearing a suit and stiff leather shoes like he'd done in high school on game days. He liked being comfortable. He didn't mind being recognized in transit and talking to fans—taking encouragement and even heckling when he was in a slump. But there was no one waiting around the platform, and when the train finally arrived, he collapsed in a seat and leaned his head against the glass, exhausted.

"Two more long balls," Johnny mumbled as he drifted. The metro lurched, vibrated, and dinged. He thought about the last three-game series of the season against Los Angeles, the final chances to clinch 500 with the pennant and wildcard races too far gone. He knew it was unlikely that he'd see more than 12 at bats—four chances per game. The train took on passengers at each stop until the seats and aisles were packed with locals and then tourists after passing through the underground chambers below Montgomery St. But Johnny was lights out—he was standing in a narrow hardware store aisle, listening to a salesman point out all the differences between locksets and deadbolts and additional protections like home security cameras to keep his family safer.

The old lady sitting beside him rubbed his leg and whispered "honey" three times before he left the hardware store. He wiped the corner of his mouth with his sweatshirt sleeve where he'd drooled and rubbed his eye sockets with the palms of his hands. "That was some nap," the old lady told him and laughed. She said he was bound to miss the ballpark and then went right into the day he got his nickname. The train was jammed with passengers standing in the aisles, holding rails above their heads to keep steady, and everyone seemed to zero in on him and her story.

Johnny loved hearing fans replay how he'd been dubbed. She told him where she and her granddaughters were sitting—upper deck, along first—when he came to home plate and cranked the first pitch straight up into the sky. Then she backtracked, describing how unusually hot and sunny it was that afternoon in the city and how the ball became lost to everyone in the bright sun, how almost no one at the park saw it come down, and kept searching the sky until a jet emerged overhead, bound for the airport. That's when the crowd roared, the old lady said. The third base umpire was holding up both arms—he'd somehow tracked the smack to deep left field, beyond the last row of bleachers—and the third base coach was signaling Johnny around the bases. She talked about how she sat in front of the television later that night to see the blast's trajectory on baseball highlights, where they replayed the footage and narration of the wound-up announcer losing sight of the ball to the sun and jetliner and telling fans that Johnny Miles must've sent that pitch on a nonstop flight out-a-here after the umpire made the call.

Johnny grinned and embraced the old lady. He thanked her for the story, for waking him up, and darted through the crammed train for the parting doors. Locals patted his back, wished him luck, told him they'd be at the game. "Back-to-back," someone shouted as the doors snapped shut. He said it back to himself on repeat as he passed through security, down a ringlet of stairs, to the underbelly of the ballpark, where he found a quiet corner in one of the locker rooms to text Clara. He asked her to call the memory care home where his mom lived and plan for someone to bring her to the game. She texted back right away, said she'd already made the call, that his mom wouldn't want to miss this.

He popped in his wireless earbuds and clicked on his Bossa Nova pre-game playlist. He let the music calm and distract his busy mind as he stretched and warmed up in the weight room. The relaxed tempos kept him from moving too fast, wasting energy. He suited up. He snacked on catered fruit and veggies, half of a ham-cheddar sandwich, a big cup of Gatorade, and waited for his group to be waived up on the field, where they took batting practice. When his turn came to hit, he asked for pitches at the corners, nothing hanging over the plate—the same locations he anticipated during the game. He listened to his smooth music and didn't try to jack anything out of the park; he focused on timing, connections, and the mechanics of his swing. There was still a lot of warming up and waiting before he could turn up the heat.

The national anthem came and went without Johnny caring who sang it. Everything went fuzzy beyond his job at the plate, his job at first base. He took to the field and skipped grounders to his teammates at second, short, and third, catching their returns on autopilot. Then everything was set in motion, and he focused on the outs as they came: pop-fly to shallow center, line-drive to third, and a strikeout to change sides. He loosened up a bit back in the dugout, trading ballcap for helmet, pulling on his batting gloves, picking out his bat. He waited, fourth in line, ready for his first shot, when his batting coach came up from behind and slapped his ass. "They're here," he said. "Your mom and wife and boys and in-laws are up in a box behind the plate."

He couldn't picture the first or second home run, but he could see himself talking with the fan who snagged his 500th homer, bargaining from the field, handing over his bat in exchange for the ball—something small to take back to his mother, waiting alongside his wife and kids on the field. Something to run her fingers against, each lace a flame of a reminder of their life together for the days she felt robbed or alone.

Q: Who won *The Twin Bill*'s 2024 Best Baseball Fiction Book?
A: Vince Wetzel, *Lose Yourself*

Illustration by Andy Lattimer

In the Outfield
By Sara Maurer

BETH OPENED THE LIFTGATE on her Suburban and the sight of the cargo area pleased her: bottled water stacked on top of Gatorade, the Yeti snug against the overnight bags, her umbrella and camping chair wedged between the cooler and wall. On top of the cooler, a container of no-bake cookies, and on top of that, a clutch of unspotted bananas.

She hefted out the cooler, slung the camping chair over her shoulder, and made her way to the outfield fence where Angie was already sitting, her feet propped against the chain link. Their routine had been the same all summer long: take Friday off work, drive the boys to the tournament, get tipsy in the outfield. Repeat Saturday. Repeat Sunday. Every summer since the boys' Little League days had passed in this way. Sometimes their husbands joined them, sometimes they didn't, but Beth and Angie were always there, knowing that if their boys looked out to the fence, they'd see their mothers there.

It was close to noon: game time. An early chance of rain had moved on and Beth stretched out her arms in front of her. "It's going to get hot now."

"Good," Angie said. "I've lost almost all my color." She opened her cooler and scooped loose ice into a tumbler, added Tito's, a slice of lemon, which she had precut at home and stored in a Ziploc bag, and topped it off with water.

Beth opened her own cooler and slid a Long Drink into a koozie. "Have you tried these yet? My new favorite."

Angie reached for the baby blue can. Her eyes opened wide. "Oh, yum."

"Take that one. I have a ton."

"Look at me. Double fisting already."

"Atta girl."

Angie took a scorebook out of her bag, a large notebook with page after page of columns and rows for keeping game stats. She started filling in the batting order.

"It's so good how you do that," Beth said.

"What, this? Oh, Josh just likes to look it over after the game. See how he did."

"Aiden would probably like it if I did that, too," Beth said. "I should learn. Looks hard."

"Nah, it's easy."

Beth watched her for a while, how she double-checked the spelling of each player's name, wrote down who the subs and pitchers were, the team names, the date, even the name of the field.

"You know what?" Beth said. "You're a good mom."

"Oh, I've just always done this."

"No, really," Beth said. "You are. A lot of moms don't even come to the games, especially at this age. I hope Josh appreciates it."

"Well, he doesn't say it, but—" Angie's voice trailed off.

"But you know it."

"Yeah, I know."

Beth picked up her phone and scrolled a while, every now and then lifting the Long Drink from the cupholder in her chair, taking a sip, and setting it down again. The sun had burned off the clouds and she squinted into the screen. "Kelly Farren travels more than any person I know," she said.

"There's a name I haven't heard in a while. Where is she?"

"Boston," Beth said. "Again."

 What's in Boston?"

"She's getting her PhD."

"Wow. Good for her, I guess."

"For sure, but this is what I don't get: If you're not going anywhere, why get this big degree? You know what I mean? We live in the Upper Peninsula. She works at this rinky-dink hospital. It's not like she's going to get this big promotion or anything."

"What's the PhD in?" Angie asked. The boys were on the field warming up. The balls made sharp, satisfying smacks when the mitts closed around them.

"Healthcare admin or something like that. But that's another thing! The hospital already has leadership. What is she doing it for?"

"Is that what she wants? To run the hospital?"

Beth raised her eyebrows. "Who knows. She already runs that whole program there. You know, the job placement program for the kids with disabilities."

"The Journey Project? That's a great program."

"Oh, don't get me wrong. It's an awesome program. Kelly gets them trained and places them with jobs. My friend's son went through it, and he's got his little job and he's doing great. She's a great person. We went to high school together. It's not that. I just don't understand: Why do it if you don't need it? If you're not getting anything out of it?"

"I always liked Kelly," Angie said.

"Oh, definitely. Me too. I've known her forever. Like I said, we graduated together."

Angie started writing again, then stopped. "Didn't Kelly work at the elementary school when the boys were there? She sometimes helped with reading."

"Yes, but she told me it wasn't challenging enough, so she decided to move on to the hospital. Now she's running that whole program and I guess it's still not enough."

"But she was very good while she was at the school, very dedicated. She's the one who got Josh the reading help."

"Oh, I'm not saying she's not dedicated. I'm not saying she's not a good person. Not at all. I'm just asking, why do you need a PhD to run a program at the county hospital when it's not even going to get you a better job or more money, you know?"

Beth picked up her phone again and began to scroll. "Looks like her husband's out there with her. Of course, she has to post about it. They make a trip out of it. She has to go out there every six months and he goes with her. It's like a whole week's vacation every six months."

Angie sipped her Tito's thoughtfully. "That'd be kind of nice though. Tom and I never do anything."

"Because we're at the field every weekend! Not that I'd want to be anywhere else, I'm just saying. Besides, she doesn't even enjoy it. It totally stresses her out. All this school and work and travel. She's stressed out all the time. And what is she getting out of it? I mean, it's got to be expensive. I don't know how they afford it."

"School's expensive," Angie said.

"It'd be different if you were guaranteed a promotion or something," Beth said. She took a long drink of her Long Drink, swallowing hard, twice, before putting the can down. "And the hospital is so small, I doubt it does tuition reimbursement. And you want to know what the worst part about it is?"

Angie looked up from the scorebook. "What?"

"Her son."

"What about her son?"

Beth waved her hands in front of her face, as though to erase the words. "Never mind. Forget I even said that. I shouldn't have. Anyway, the game's about to start."

"No, right. Of course," Angie said. She recorded the official game start time in the scorebook.

Their boys jogged onto the field. Tall, quick-footed boys. Almost men. Their plucky teenage biceps shone in the sun. Both were outfielders, Aiden in left field, Josh in center, which was why Beth and Angie sat where they did. It was important for the boys to know they were there rooting them on. That and, behind the outfield fence, no one made a fuss about the coolers. In the moments before the first pitch, Beth slid a new Long Drink into her koozie, and Angie freshened her Tito's.

Beth sank back in her chair and dropped her sunglasses over her eyes. She smiled over at Angie. "See? We could be in Boston right now, but would you want to miss a single minute of this? They're only kids once."

"Exactly," Angie said. She recorded the first few pitches. A ball, a strike swinging, another ball.

"Be ready out there, Aiden," Beth called. If he heard her, he didn't let on.

The pitcher threw another strike and Angie recorded it. "So, you've known Kelly a long time, then?"

"Oh, God yes. Since we were 12. I wasn't trying to talk bad about her. I hope you don't think that. The Journey Project is great. It's just that everyone thinks she's this really great person—and I do, too, in some ways—but when you look at what kind of mom she is—" Beth shook her head. "It's sad."

"But she has such a positive impact on all those Journey Project kids!" Angie tipped back her Tito's. She missed the next pitch, a strikeout, and didn't bother to record it.

"Oh, everyone thinks she's so amazing, and dedicated, like you said, but they don't know the full story. Not like I do. I know her mom, her whole family. I've known them forever."

"You must be close."

Beth sat up. "Well, we were, but—I feel bad talking about people."

"Oh, totally."

Angie lifted her pencil, ready to start recording again. "Was that a strikeout looking or swinging?"

"Looking," Beth said. And then, "But her son, well, you know he has a disability, too, right?"

"No! I didn't know that!"

"Severe. Absolutely sweet kid though. He's the reason she got into her line of work in the first place. But here she is, working and working, moving from one job to the next, going all over the country for this Ph.D. that she doesn't even need, taking her husband with her and making trips out of it, sightseeing and all that, and who do you think is taking care of their son while they're gone?"

Angie set her pencil down and closed the scorebook. "He's not left on his own, is he?"

"Her mother! Her poor mother who's got to be, what, in her seventies? Taking care of that boy who's just as big as ours, maybe bigger. She has to move into Kelly's house for the week to keep an eye on him. Make his meals. Clean up after him, and God knows what else. I'm not even sure he can use the bathroom without help. Can you imagine? And Kelly tells me that taking care of that boy is what keeps her mother going. As if her mother has no other reason for living than taking care of that boy. All so that someday everyone has to call her Dr. Farren."

"I had no idea!" Angie said. She sat quietly for a moment, eyes drifting slowly over the outfield, her tumbler drooping in her hand. "I always liked Kelly," she said.

"Well, now you know the full story. And I'm not out to turn people against her, it's just hard knowing what I know when everyone thinks she's so great. We were in the same work co-op program in high school, you know. We had classes in the morning and then worked at the real estate office in the afternoon. She was always bumming rides from me. Not many people have known her as long as me. Wait, did you want another one of these?"

Beth dug a Long Drink out of her cooler and held it out to Angie, dripping and cold in the afternoon light.

Angie took it and drank. Her eyes hovered on the gold cuff around Beth's wrist. "That's beautiful," she said, turning Beth's wrist to examine it. "Is it new?"

"Oh, thanks," Beth said, smiling down at the interlocking yellow bands. "I just hit 25 years at the real estate office. Can you believe it? I practically run that place now."

"Oh wow," Angie said. "Twenty-five years. Congrats."

"Thanks." She slipped off the cuff to read the engraving. "It says, 'With many thanks.'"

"Good for you," Angie said.

Just then, a crack exploded from the batter's box and the other team's parents stood in the stands and cheered, watching as the ball soared wide and weightless, like a kite caught in a perfect current of air.

Aiden studied the path of the ball, feet already in motion, shuffling toward his mother, then running, flying.

"Fence!" Josh shouted. "Fence!"

Beth watched Aiden come to her, the beauty of his movement as his body responded to the lightning calculations of his brain. He leaped against the fence, a long backward stretch, almost in her lap, closed his mitt around the ball, and held it.

"Yes, Aiden!" Beth screamed. She had stopped breathing, and now she kicked at the fence, rattling it, splashing her drink on her thigh. Then she was on her feet, hopping like a child, and Angie hopped with her. They clapped hands and patted Aiden's back and head.

"Let's go!" Beth shouted. "Let's go!"

With easy movements, almost lazy, Aiden tossed the ball to the shortstop and trotted back to his position. But then he turned back to Beth and waved. His smile was big and white, a little bashful. The sunlight had turned long and gold, drenching everything in beauty, and Beth stood completely still, her breath coming back to her at last. *I am here and I am thankful,* she thought. *I am so thankful.*

"Meet the" Vignettes

Sara Maurer

Who are you?

I'm a writer in the Upper Peninsula of Michigan, where we get about two months of baseball/softball weather each year.

What was the inspiration for your piece?

During my son's baseball tournament, I went on a walk between games and listened to an old episode of The New Yorker Fiction podcast: Sam Lipsyte reading John Purdy's story, "About Jessie Mae," where two women discuss a woman they claim to hate but whom they are sick with jealousy of. When the next game started, I sat in the outfield with the other moms, and they started talking about another mom. It was like Jessie Mae coming to life. The story almost wrote itself.

What's your favorite team?

Sault Area High School Blue Devils! Professional would have to be the Tigers.

What's your favorite baseball memory?

I have a lifetime of memories, but one of my favorites is when my husband and I took our daughter to her first Tigers game when she was a baby. I don't remember anything specific about the game, just that the whole day was draped in sunshine. We got her a little pink Tigers baseball cap, and she ate ice cream out of a token Tigers helmet, which we kept for the longest time. Now, she plays Division II softball. What a journey.

What's the highlight of your writing career?

The highlight of my writing career was in 2020, when I finally decided to focus on having a writing career. I enrolled in the Stanford Continuing Studies novel writing program, and for the next two years, I focused on the craft of writing. I've never felt so happy or so scared. Eventually, I signed with an agent, and in 2024, St. Martin's Press picked up my debut novel, *A Good Animal*, for publication in the winter of 2026.

What's your favorite baseball book?

"The Cactus League" by Emily Nemens.

Q: How many short stories did *The Twin Bill* publish in their first 16 issues?

A: 90

Illustration by Elliot Lin

Hope in Baseball
By Clayton Bradshaw-Mittal

IN THE LOCKER ROOM before the final game of the season, our team gathers around the soon-to-be fired manager who tells us that there is no hope in baseball, that money rules the game and the only teams destined for championships are those who can afford better players than the ones standing in front of him today. He takes a wooden bat, swings it at the metal supports holding the ceiling above our heads. The thud of the bat echoes dense in our bones. He swings again and again, quicker and quicker, until the wood cracks into a deep stain the length of the bat and again and again until the bat disintegrates into a thousand splintered shreds. He tosses the bat into an empty laundry bin and walks into the dark tunnel that leads to the field. We look at one another, our eyes fogged with the exhaustion of a losing season, shrug our shoulders, pick up our gloves off the benches, and walk out behind him.

The horizon glows orange through the chain link fence atop the hill at the other end of the stadium, the last pulsating crescent of the sun gasping just beyond our view. Barely legible dust floats through the humid air, chokes us, and the sweat begins to cool against our skin. It will be dark soon, and, despite our manager's pessimism, despite the weight of our cleats sticking into the too-soft soil, despite our red, dry eyes from months of traveling across the country on a chartered jet airplane with duct tape stretched across a seam of the left wing, we are excited.

Our wooden bats make whoosh sounds in the air as we practice our swings, and the smacks of balls hitting leather gloves echo in the silence of dusk. The air chills. Our shoulders thaw. The first spectators trickle in; the fizz of beer and conversation drips in the stadium seats. The stands are full, though we don't deserve a crowd, no matter how cleanly bleached the bases might be and neatly the chalk of the foul line has been poured. We suppose they've come to watch our dying heaves as we dissolve into the basements of the official record books. Our season will be over tonight, tucked into popular memory as the most losses suffered by a team in over a century, but playing here on this day, as in any ballpark on any day, is the dream we dreamt as children, tucked away in our beds, listening as televisions and battery-operated AM radios blared for our parents, for our grandparents, for our aunties and our uncles, Game Seven home runs and high-pressure strikeouts and sports show highlights from the first perfect game pitched in years.

We pile into the dugout and take our seats on the bench. Riley turns his cap around backward, and shotguns a Dr. Pepper he's snuck into the game. He calls it a tradition. I've done this the last game of every season since Little League, he says and sits, legs splayed, next to Ortega. Petrie pours a cup of Gatorade on the ground, the stream of liquid painting a sad face into the dirt layered thin over the smooth concrete. He points to the face, says it's art, but the batting coach tells him a sad face is not art just because Petrie's wife caught him with his dick inside an Uber driver's mouth and packed her bags; it's a slipping hazard that needs to be cleaned up.

And kneeling, head bowed over the bench behind the manager, Alarcón rubs his fingers back and forth over a turquoise-beaded rosary, the Virgin Mary hidden under his thumb. Slater asks him why he bothers with superstition, even a win won't do anything for them, but Alarcón replies that his faith in Mary's virginity lends him undying hope in the game we all play.

The tension flows in waves amongst fans and players alike. We know the other team is still upset at us for beaning their right fielder a month ago with a poorly aimed fastball, an accident near the end of the game when our pitcher Vega's arm had turned spongy after eight innings without the other team registering a single hit and twisted on the release and the ball had slipped through the sweat dripping down to his fingers before thudding into a batter's chest, and while we feel their anger at this slip is justified, we are ready, according to the unspoken bylaws of baseball tradition, to dispute their inevitable, required response.

In front of the cage protecting the fans, the umpire says play ball and the opposing pitcher stands in a firm stance, legs slightly apart, looking between the catcher's legs to see what pitch the catcher wants him to throw. But this decision, this pitch, begins with a conversation. The pitcher shakes his head at the first sign he's given. We believe he's refusing to start the game with a curveball. We know he wants to intimidate us, frighten us with something fast, something straight down the middle. This is a game driven by broken masculinity, where the old men still playing, still coaching, believe in a show of force to terrorize their opponents like they're generals rampaging through the countryside.

It seems a quarter of the stadium has risen to their feet, expecting the fight to come early, to erupt sooner rather than later, and it dawns on us the only reason they've come to see the shit show of a team we've become, more than the free bobblehead doll in Ortega's likeness with every purchase of an eight dollar beer and twelve dollar hotdog, is to witness the moment we finally collapse into pre-diluvian brutality. The few fans we've kept have lost hope for home-run races, for outfielders catching fly balls just as they tumble into the crowd, their lower backs crashing into low walls, for walk-off triples that drive in winning runs that sear into the hippocampus of every ten-year-old whose grandfather ever took them out to a game.

The pitcher winds up, brings his glove to his face, nearly kissing the leather housing for his thumb. He draws his front leg into his body and leans onto his back foot before pushing his entire body into a one-meter step forward, his right arm following the motion like a trebuchet until the ball releases parallel to the ground at the height of his eyeballs. The ball speeds through the air, just a little higher than the shoulder of our first baseman, Phillips, who has stepped up to bat, who refuses to swing because he's played this game long enough to see a ball too high above the strike zone before it even leaves a pitcher's hand. On the next pitch, another fastball, this one right in the middle of the strike zone, Phillips hits the ball high and arching into the glove of the right fielder.

This is the moment, as we keep our focus on the field, that Petrie walks backward over his own drawing and trips on a discarded plastic cup that's fallen from the stands above us, and his head bangs hard against the concrete floor. The batting coach checks to make sure he's okay, and when Petrie nods, the coach pulls him up, tells him, that's what you get for acting like a little sad boy over something that's very clearly your fault.

Another batter. Another pitch. Another video on the scoreboard of the mascot tipping over a stadium railing after being pushed by a half-drunk fan whose marriage proposal has just been rebuffed. We spend a moment, eyes glued to the stadium's big screen television, marveling at how often this happens. This time, the pitcher throws too far inside, nearly clipping the lint hanging from Ortega's chin. We stand up from the bench, ready to rush the field, ready to protect one of our own like Barbary lions, teeth flashing and claws extended, closing in around a cub to protect them. If the other team retaliates here, if they hit Ortega with a pitch now, we will have no choice but to respond in force, in anger, in a flash flood of cherry-eyed violence.

That is the only way such rivalries end with any degree of satisfaction. Retaliation breeds retaliation and crimson marks the shape of a baseball's seam are left imprinted on the bridge of a broken nose which breeds another retaliation until the hostility overflows into a fight on the field. And our collected anxiety tells us that this fight will happen here today. After all, tomorrow, we will be home, ready to watch the playoffs from our posh, pleather couches, some of us never to return to this stadium unless in another team's uniform.

The pitcher's eyes, like polished porcelain in the shadow of his cap's bill, moves towards us, seeming to take stock of our standing posture in the dugout, even as the rest of his face angles forward. The next pitch stays on target, through the middle of the strike zone, slaps against the oil of the catcher's glove. Ortega does not flinch. On the next throw, the ball curves right, and Ortega drills the ball into the left field wall. Ground rule double. We advance to second base.

Alarcón kisses his rosary. Slater kisses Alarcón. Petrie says he used to kiss his wife like that. The batting coach hands Petrie a beer and slaps his ass.

Ortega takes a few steps towards third base, widens his legs into a modified sprinter's stance, his shoulders squared in the direction of the pitcher. When Spears steps up to the plate, Ortega hops another inch or two toward third, prompting the pitcher to throw the ball to the second baseman, but Ortega's already there, already safe, before the second baseman can tag him out. Ortega stands, brushes the dirt off his uniform with gloved hands, takes only a single step towards third base this time but blows a kiss to the catcher who hasn't taken his eyes off Ortega.

The pitcher finally throws a pitch to Spears. Low fastball. Spears doesn't swing. The umpire ticks the miniature device in his hand to count the ball as outside the strike zone, and Spears takes a step back, holds his bat against the forehead of his helmet, closes his eyes, mouths a prayer. Through the loose fit of his jersey, we can see his shoulders relax. He's another old pro who's remained in just enough shape to keep himself from demotion back to the minor leagues. He won a championship with Houston a few years back and doesn't care about winning another one. Spears is the kind of athlete who wants to keep playing until his lower back grinds itself into a wheelchair on his last swing, and the way his spine has been popping lately, we wonder if that last swing, that final grinding rotation, will be here on this field today. Not that any of us believe he'll go down without a fight.

The next pitch is when it happens. When the ball appears to slip and leaves the pitcher's knuckles with a wobble through the ambient dust and stadium light into the base of the blue number seven on Spears' back. We watch

Spears' body arch upwards and his shoulder blades fold inward and we run on the field, the dust rising further to obscure our advance.

We find ourselves in a clogged mass of sweaty bodies and discarded red shirts and bloodied fists. The skin on Ortega's forehead has torn and will need stitches later, but in this moment, our collective knuckles scraping along high cheekbones, deep into a season of missteps and awkwardly missed swings, we feel like the baseball team we've trained to be, telegraphing our blurred fists into the other team's teeth and stomping the mud off our cleats onto freshly mangled players, because one of our own has been hurt and the only way we know to express empathy, to show our solidarity, is to punish the other team as though we are mounting a teenage revolt, as though we imagine them to be the parents who dragged our kicking childhood selves away from the soil of broken fields when the night sky grew dark and celestially spotted, the parents who grew upset and beat us with thick leather belts whenever the rain fell in spring and we slid between the bases through the mud, tearing holes in the formerly sterile white pants they'd bought us just for games and practices (or for some of us our only remaining pair of intact blue jeans), and tonight we don't care about the fines or getting booted from the game because we believe that in these moments, under the immortalizing rays of the field lights, the world peers into our baseball diamond to forget its problems for only a moment, just so it may focus on us playing our little game, to record how lost we find ourselves when fighting our miniscule battles under the bright lights of summer and spring, to escape the struggles of love lost and pain found, to live vicariously through our contests on fields they wish they could inhabit, to seek out hope in an eternal sport. After all, this game is not really ours. We only play it.

We know we'll go home tonight, our collective identity shattered at season's end. Spears will be demoted to the minor leagues, his age beginning to slow down his swing. Ortega will be traded to the Red Sox for two outfielders who will never step into the starting lineup and a draft pick slated for sometime in the future. Phillips will stay on for some degree of continuity going into spring. Other players will leave or stay or leave only return seasons down the road. Alarcón will be arrested for trying to smuggle an unvaccinated cat from the Dominican Republic. Jackson will be blacklisted from the league after a pitching coach discovers steroids and a semiautomatic pistol in his locker during a preseason practice. And I will be here in this stadium for another season because I've never been particularly good at the business side of baseball (the result of growing up too poor, without any money to learn how to manage), nor do I desire to be, and my lucky bat never fits in my luggage when I move. This team may be dead, ashes thrown into the off-season wind, but what I really want is to be part of its successor, one of the atoms pulled together to make up the molecules of the next iteration, to be a borrowed organ in the next Frankenstein-esque baseball body of this team, to take part in the next round of a Sisyphean pursuit of the playoffs.

The fight's over. Ortega and the other team's pitcher have been ejected, and the manager has left the game on his own accord, giving up on us before our final at-bat. On my way back to the dugout, I pick up the ball that beaned Spears and rotate it slowly in my hand until I can slip it into the plastic grocery bag of snacks I've left hanging near the tunnel door. Before I hide the ball away, I ask Spears to sign it, and he laughs before scribbling half his name, then asks why I want it. I say nothing and smile because he would never believe it's because I still believe in this team, in what being part of what we've done together, what we will do in the few innings left to come.

Because, even in the closing exhales of an expiring season, I still dream of baseball, and others dream for us. Even if we are losing this game by ten runs, a few good hits in the last inning can land us a win and brighten the day of a teenager who's about to get caught playing hooky from school, hold an oil worker breathless on his hour-long drive home through the West Texas desert, push two old soldiers closer together in their seats at dive bar somewhere in Dallas until their boots hook around one another's. We might even tie it all up, take this game to overtime, extend the season by another inning or two. But no matter what, when tonight is over, there will be hope for next year.

***

The air is cold for an early Arlington October as I walk out the stadium doors well past midnight. Petrie's puking into the dumpster. His beer comes back up yellow, steaming, smelling like warm bile. Alarcón pulls a blanket from the backseat of his car, wraps it around Petrie's shoulders to keep him from a case of hypothermia. I consider offering to drive Petrie home, but his wife's absence means he will guilt me into staying there while he downs a few beers, asks me about the last time I sucked another man's cock, wants to know if I'll suck his. Boundaries are not Petrie's strong suit, nor is self-control. Besides, he'll say, it's not like we have practice or a game tomorrow.

I would tell him that I do, that my low orbit around baseball means I cannot halt in my life's rotation around the sport for fear of crashing down to an Earth with real-world realities I do not wish to face, that I will be in the

161

weight room tomorrow morning and at the batting cages by afternoon, that I will write out imagined batting orders for the team we could be next season while *Bull Durham* streams across my television. I have become a priest of my sport, celibate, studying, proselytizing. I want to be a conduit between the fans and the crack of a baseball bat because I've nothing else of quality to give. Besides, I'd tell him, in that moment his hand grazes the front of my pants, I prefer my men with coarse hair poking from underneath the top button of their shirts.

At home, I rub my thumb across the stitched seam of the baseball with Spears' autograph, toss it in the air a few times. There's a dent where the spike from someone's cleat nearly pierced the ball and the dirt has mixed with sweat to turn it a dirty beige. A memory of a moment from the fight when I slipped on the ball and landed on my ass next to the pitcher's mound connects to another of Phillips throwing his helmet at someone, missing, the helmet hitting my leg. My right hamstring suddenly feels hollow and numb, tomorrow's soreness radiating along the edges. I turn on the television to highlights of the fight, listen to the alternating highs and lows of the talking head's voice.

A trash year, the talking head enunciates, concludes in yet another dumpster fire, and the talking head says he cannot look away. But he has faith, he claims, that this team will rebuild and come back strong next season.

I can't help but agree about the bad season, about the magnetism of such flame-outs. Mostly I agree that *we*, whatever iteration *we* return in, will grow beyond the bad year the old *we* just endured. Even when there's no hope left, I still believe. I still aspire. I still drag my feet forward across the powdered red clay of the infield around the bases and toward home plate.

My thumb rests on the dent in the ball and suddenly I remember why I want it.

Because I'm playing the game I played as a child, and, as for so many others, the sandlots of home were the first step in buying a lottery ticket to a journey out of the soul-sucking poverty of my youth.

Because, as I switch channels to watch Kevin Costner smash home run after home run to a narrator who reminds his audience that no one will ever remember the minor league home run record of Costner's record, I remember that no one will think of me tomorrow and anonymity is a necessary silhouette while waiting to be overtaken by golden flames on a new horizon.

Because no matter the pain, the drama, the absolute shit day I've had, there's always just a tiny sliver of hope rooted in the green grass and loose dirt of a baseball field.

Q: Who won *The Twin Bill*'s 2023 Best Baseball Fiction Book?
A: Mark Stevens, *The Fireballer*

"Meet the" Vignettes
Clayton Bradshaw-Mittal

Who are you?

I am a queer, previously unhoused veteran turned writer and professor. Originally from Texas, I now live in Erie, Pennsylvania and teach Creative Writing at Gannon University.

What was the inspiration for your piece?

I've always believed in the democracy of baseball. Essentially, until the final moments of a game—the final strike pitched, a walk-off home run, etc.—there is always a chance to rally and win. As a Texas Rangers fan, I remember being on the wrong side of this when they lost the 2011 World Series despite being one strike away from winning the whole thing in Game Six. So, in the deepest, darkest moments of my life, I always returned to baseball as a reminder that things could turn around. And, when I began writing, I held onto this idea (title included) of a story about retaining hope even when all is lost. And when I began working on one of my current book projects, I thought of this story as an antidote to Don DeLillo's *Underworld*. Where that novel begins in a moment of baseball glory, I wanted mine to begin mired in the sort of failure from which life truly emerges.

What's your favorite team?

I have been a Texas Rangers fan my entire life. My grandfather was a railroad worker in northwest Texas, and my earliest happy memories were of him sitting on his back porch smoking a cigar with the Texas Rangers playing on the radio.

Who is your favorite player?

Currently, I am a huge fan of Adolis García. He is a great hitter with a brutal swing. And he has so much flair. I love watching him play.

What's your favorite baseball memory?

As much as I shouldn't like this moment for all its machismo and toxicity, I have spent my entire life thinking about and romanticizing Nolan Ryan's altercation with Robin Ventura in 1993. I watched it on TV with my grandfather two weeks before my seventh birthday, and I was already a big Nolan Ryan fan. At the time, he was 46, on the verge of retirement, and still throwing so very hard. Ryan was the epitome of Texas spirit, handling Ventura like a stray bull. And when the dust cleared and Ventura was ejected, Ryan just brushed it off and kept pitching. There's something so Texan about that. About how despite all the issues surrounding the incident and how much Ryan's bones likely ached, he just kept moving.

What's the highlight of your writing career?

I had a story in *Story* last winter. It's such a good journal, and Michael Nye is a brilliant editor. In addition, it was the first story I wrote after defending my dissertation, and really validated the direction I was moving in my work.

Favorite baseball movie?

I'm going to go with *Bull Durham* here. It's a great exploration of the sexuality and complicated masculinity inherent in baseball. Plus, Kevin Costner was really hitting all those home runs in the movie. No stunt professionals or tricks of the camera. Just Costner hitting the ball and calling them dingers.

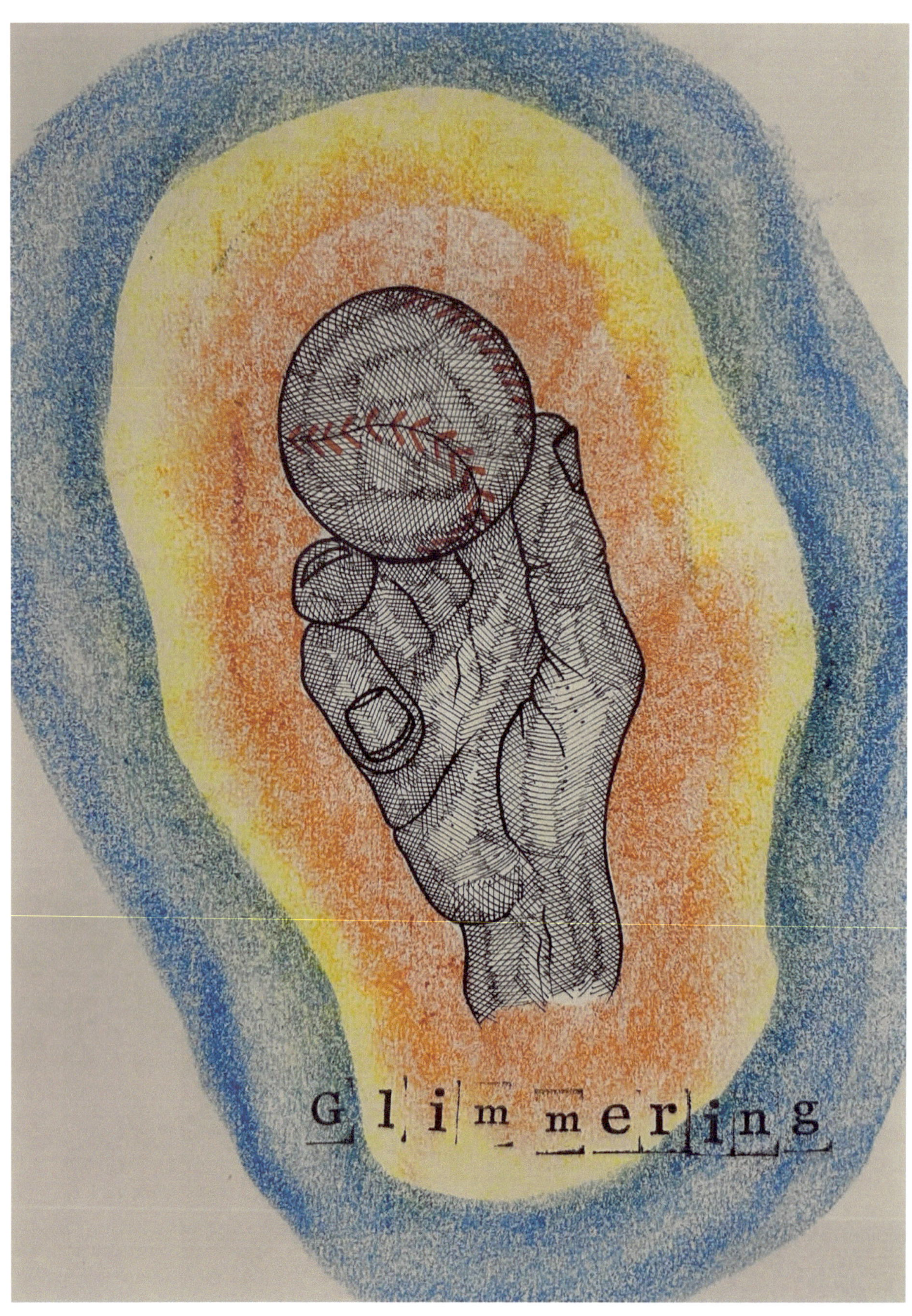

Illustration by Matt Lawrence

Glimmering
By Lindsay Borden

SLUMPED ON THE BENCH, sitting back on your tailbone, spitting out sunflower shells, jawin' and chawin', taking in the game. That was Randy Little's idea of heaven, and he had already spent an eternity there. His playing days were so long gone they were like somebody else's youth. Could that slender left-hander really have been him? Seems unlikely. That fiery, mediocre pitcher who'd blown out his arm early and reinvented himself as a fair-to-middling fielder—him? In his mind, he saw that scrappy young player so clear. Kind of tenderly, too, almost like a son. Heck, anymore, like a grandson. No, no—more like someone else's grandkid—someone close, but not bone close. Fact was, when he thought back over his childhood idols, those ballplayers he'd grown up rooting for, well, there he was, his own young self, taken his place among them. Not the best of them, not near. More like that guy you pulled for and hoped for and more often than not ended up shaking your head over, or nearly falling over backwards when he actually came through.

Then had come all those years of coaching and managing and coaching again, those years he'd put together and added on to what he'd learned in years of watching and waiting and soaking the game up right into his flesh. He was soggy with it now, boy. Baseball knowledge practically oozed from him, but the more that seeped out, the more he absorbed. I must have seen it all, he thought, but there's always more to see. If you keep your eyes open.

Long years—decades now—of growing up and growing old in a boy's game. And maybe he couldn't remember exactly what year it was that he had struck out the side on nine pitches, or had grounded out to short in the bottom of the ninth in that game against New York. Maybe he couldn't remember exactly if a rookie Marcus Smith had been playing for Boston or Detroit that time he'd been caught in a rundown that must've lasted a good minute and a half. But Little remembered clear as anything that high meaty fastball he'd got away with to Powell, before reaching back and finishing him off with an 0-and-2 sinker. Remembered standing in against Nichols, that year he won Cy Young and MVP, whenever that was, and knowing the cutter was coming and still getting jammed up and in, feeling the jolt of his bat splintering, and starting down the line holding what was left of the handle and knowing he'd been flummoxed yet again, but this time by one of the best there was. He could almost feel his blood pound, thinking of standing on the dugout steps and screaming, "Tag him! Tag him! Tag him! Tag him!" as if his fielders weren't trying their damnedest to do just that, while Smith danced back and forth between them like a boy, grinning and sparking, as if there were no dark years of illness and addiction and poverty ahead of him, as if he had all the time in the world to dance along the base path, driving the infield to distraction and the crowd to its feet.

Clear as water, clear and shining like a shard of glass, glinting like ice, layer on layer of memory. The sweet swing of Inohito glimmering fathoms down below the sweet swing of Jordan, the galloping stride of Masterson echoing length for length the galloping grace of Bonds. Speaker Jones stealing second over the headfirst slide of Henderson, on top of the belly-flopping swoosh of...who was that, way down deep? Sneaking in under the tag? Down there, in the shadows?... Scrappy little Randy Little, will ya look at that. No wonder Little's old eyes glittered, beneath their sleepy lids.

"Bring 'em in, you think, Gopher?"

"Nah, Kendy. This kid can't bunt. Hands ain't soft enough. They're only bluffin'."

Mover kept his infield back, and after two failed bunt attempts, the kid at the plate lined straight to Jones and into the double play.

Illustration by Neon Black Tiger

Interviews

Illustration by Jason David Córdova

Darryl Strawberry
By Scott Bolohan

This interview was first published in December 2020.

My first baseball glove was a brown Rawlings. I can remember going with my dad to Sports Authority to pick it out. My fingers barely reached past the palm of the glove. And on that palm was the facsimile signature of Darryl Strawberry.

I was five when I got the glove, and I don't think I could have told you much about Strawberry other than that he was in the Major Leagues and good enough to have his signature on my glove. So naturally, I wanted to be like him.

When he joined the Yankees after serving a suspension for cocaine use, I was at his first game with the team on August 4, 1995. I remember a buzz around Tiger Stadium watching him take batting practice. Well out of his prime, he still had that star power that only a handful have had in baseball history. Years later, he signed a baseball for me before a game and I remember thinking how tall he was, his 6'6" frame dwarfed me as a kid who literally looked up to him. He was bigger than the game.

I always knew there was a darker side to him, that he had struggled with his demons ever since he was in the spotlight.

After his playing career ended, most pictures I saw of Strawberry were him in court wearing an orange prison jumpsuit. There was a stretch of every few years where something else would pop up in the news about the trouble he was in. So often these stories have a tragic ending, and I don't think it would have surprised anyone if that was Strawberry's fate as well.

And then, I heard nothing about him.

It turns out I had been missing an incredible story. I didn't hear about him getting sober. I didn't hear about him becoming a minister. I didn't hear about him dedicating his life to helping others.

I spoke on Zoom with Strawberry about his latest book, *Turn Your Season Around*. Far from his days as an egotistic baseball star, Strawberry was soft-spoken and humble. He talked about how in normal years, he would have been traveling the country preaching to people who are hurting and "so fearful that somebody might know they have problems." Darryl doesn't shy away from his past struggles and says people "will come tell me their problems after they hear me speak because I'm sharing everything that I overcame."

We talked about his life on and off the field and how he hopes his book can inspire people—just as he did with a 5-year-old with a brand-new baseball glove.

When did you start writing this book?

I started writing this book way before the pandemic, even before I even knew COVID-19 would be a season where we would all be stuck. The book was written way before that. I picked the title way back then, and they said, 'Well, what do you what are your ideas about writing a book?' I said, 'Well, I think is for people that will have to turn their season around—we always have to turn our season around.'

I was kind of using it like playing baseball, in the sense of you have 80 games in the first half of the season, and you could be in a slump. A lot of times, things like that happened during the course of a season. The media would write things saying, 'Well, he's not going to have a good year,' but they forgot there was a whole second half of the season, there were 80 more ballgames left. They don't understand that you don't cut the season off. It's like the life that we've been living for the last six months, but you still have another six months to bring joy to your season where you can finish up strong. Little did I know that we would all be in the season that we would have to look to turn it around in some kind of way.

It sounds like you are doing better than ever.

Better than ever. Better than ever playing baseball, better than ever hitting home runs, better than championships, better than making millions of dollars, better than ever. You find such a great joy and reward for having peace with God. At the end of the day, I'm a sinner, I'm a heathen who was broken and lost and living in sin. And I was separated from God, and God's Spirit came to me, and not only did he give me grace, he gave me his gift to utilize this platform to reach others. I think that's incredible that your mess becomes his message to other people.

I think a lot of times people don't realize that, because everybody's pointing at people's issues. We don't know why people have struggles, we don't know where people are coming from. Some of us do actually get on the other side. I've had a transformation in my life with God and submitted myself and surrendered my life and basically turned away from all the worldly things.

I think a lot of fans view your career as sort of a wasted opportunity. But from the perspective that you have now, how do you view your baseball career? Did that help set you up for what was to come?

No question it did. They're looking at a wasted opportunity from a natural perspective. God was looking at it from the supernatural. He was looking at it from the long term, not the short term. They were looking at the Hall of Fame. The Hall of Fame really means nothing at the end of the day, because had I stayed on that course, I probably would have made another $50-$60 million playing baseball, and I probably would have never met Jesus. I probably would have never had the relationship and understanding I have today and wouldn't live by real biblical principles. I know something that they don't understand because I lived it. There were a bunch of yes-people that said, 'You can live any kind of way.' But when I entered in into this relationship, He said, 'Well, you can't live this way.' He's very easy going about you living according to the right way that's going to make you better and that's what we all really want. At the end of my life, I'm not going to have to answer to man, I'm going to have to answer to God. And I think so many people are going to miss that part because they're so focused on right now. And then they don't ever think twice about the end.

So, many fans probably think that way, too. 'Oh, he had missed opportunities,' no, now I got the greatest seat that you can ever imagine. Remember, fans were cheering for me when I was playing, and I'm always grateful for fans, I love fans, and I appreciate fans. But the gift that God has given me to go and minister to people and win souls and see people come down to the altar on the altar call, and weeping and crying and their life is being changed—that is the ultimate dream a person can ever have.

You talk a lot about the importance of taking off your baseball uniform. In your book you say, "My uniform was merely a facade for greatness, shielding the brokenness that ached within me." When did you realize that? And how did that change?

I think you realize that when you're playing. You saw a few players who played at the highest level. I got a chance to see a guy like Gary Carter live an abundant life in the uniform. I got a chance to see a guy like Mookie Wilson live an abundant life in a uniform. I can't say that about many people. But I can say I saw a few people living in my time because their life was different, their life was not the uniform. There was something special about the way they lived and what they cared about. The uniform was just a part of who they were. When I was wearing the uniform, the uniform was who I was. And once I took the uniform off, I really understood that I had the wrong identity. I was identifying myself as what everybody saw me as and what the media was projecting I should be. I was trying to live as what they wanted me to be instead of who God wanted me to be. And that's the difference. I saw the lifestyle that those players lived. They didn't have egos. They weren't prideful, they didn't boast, they didn't run around with women, they didn't go out and drink and they didn't go out and party. That's what a real man is all about. You see real character from that. I just wasn't there to be able to receive that at that time.

There's another moment in the book where you talk about hitting the home run in Game 7 and you said you didn't even really enjoy it. What did you learn from that experience?

The hype of everything can really get to you, especially when you're an everyday player and your star on the team, you're just consumed with so much media attention to focus on you, 'Are you going to do better?' It's just so much that goes into it. And when you finally reach that point, and you achieve all that, and then you say, 'Okay, who am I? What's next?' Because that's only going to last for so long. A lot of times you only remember athletes for what they did last. Then you play again next year, and you make a mistake, and then everybody else has something to say about you. You can't live in the past and that happens with so many great athletes, they always want to scream about 'he's not this, he's not that' and when you take the uniform off, who are you? Just because you have all these earthly things, who are you in these earthly things because one day all that's going to be so old to you. Then that emptiness on the inside of you that's never been filled by the right stuff, God Himself makes you search from the outside for everything.

I didn't want to be in the headlines anymore. I wanted to be a man like those that I've learned from, like Moses and Peter. They all had issues, but they found a way to walk with God. I learned that God loves a man that has some type of humility about himself and no ego. Because egos are big, that's a three-letter word 'ego'—Easing God Out. You ease God right out, and you play God yourself. And so I just didn't really want to be that person anymore, I just really wanted to find a different road to life. Finding that road to life was not easy. It was a very difficult challenge. But my wife, Tracy, she helped me find the way. She was the one that really said to me, 'When are you going to finally take off that uniform and figure out who you are?' And I was completely blown away by that—it was a real statement. Everybody else was following me and slapping me on the back saying, 'You're great, you're great.' She says, 'When are you going to take the uniform off and really find out who you are as a man?' That's when the change came about.

Was that a turning point for you?

That was really a turning point. I mean, because she helped me get past the uniform. Because if you can't get past the uniforms, the trophies, the success—and a lot of guys can't. That's why they stay around it, because they can't get away from the game. It's all that they know, it's all that they've done the whole life. I did the same thing. People ask me all the time, 'Why don't you coach, you have so much wisdom and knowledge?' I probably do. But I needed to remove myself from that. And God was calling me to a bigger picture.

Q: How many home runs have been hit by people interviewed in *The Twin Bill*?

A: 778 (Darryl Strawberry - 335, Willie Horton - 325, Ed Kranepool - 118)

Illustration by Mark Bolohan

Faye Webster
By Scott Bolohan

This interview was first published in July 2021.

Faye Webster is having a breakout year.

After her song "Better Distractions" was included on Barack Obama's year-end playlist in December, Webster's fourth album, *I Know I'm Funny haha* was released on June 25, 2021, and named Best New Music by *Pitchfork*. It's parts country, folk, and R&B, with a certain timeless quality, yet only could have been made now.

The 23-year-old Atlanta native is also a huge baseball fan, selling baseball-themed merch and often wearing her Braves gear. The new album features the song "A Dream With a Baseball Player" about the crush she developed on Atlanta Braves star Ronald Acuna Jr, featuring lyrics like, "I could just meet him and get it over/Or I'll just keep wearing his name on/My shirt."

And that she did.

The Braves invited her to sing "Take Me Out to the Ballgame" during the 7th inning on April 11, 2019, and she got to meet Acuna Jr. before the game. We spoke to her about Acuna Jr. a few days before his 2021 season-ending injury.

Proving her album title correct, Webster had us laughing throughout our conversation, which touched on the Braves, flaming baseball bats, and what makes a good walk-up song.

"A Dream With a Baseball Player" is about Ronald Acuna Jr. How did you become a fan?

I kind of just grew up with the Braves. I was a kid and Atlanta going to Braves games. I feel like it was just something my family always did. So I was always a fan. But yeah, I think it was like 2018, 2019, and I was just really, really invested. I wasn't touring as much, I was living home alone, and I just spent what felt like every breathing second being into the Braves those two years.

How did you end up meeting him?

I was talking about baseball in a *Pitchfork* interview and this person DM'd me on Twitter. He was just like, 'Hey, read your *Pitchfork* article, I work for marketing with the Braves and I would love to talk to you.' And I looked at this person's profile and he had like, 17 followers and I was very skeptical. So I looked up his name and, sure enough, he definitely does [work for the Braves]. He was just like, 'I think it'd be so cool if you sang at the game next week,' like it was something very spontaneous. And I was like, 'Yes, please.' I thought that was kind of the only mission. And he did mention I could go to batting practice before the game and watch on the field. I was like, 'Okay, yeah, of course.' That's when he was like, 'Okay, he's ready to meet you.' I was like, 'Who?' Nobody really told me about this. After batting practice when everybody went to the locker room, they made him stay. They introduced me to him and he had his translator who was really cool. His name is Franco [Garcia]. He does a bunch of stuff with the Braves. And I just talked to him for like, three minutes. And then we took a picture and he's like, 'See ya' and never thought about me again.

I've seen those pictures of you two. What do you talk about in a situation like that?

I was really nervous. And at the point where he wasn't really that fluent in English. So you know, I'm sure anything I said to him I was just rambling. But I was like, 'Hey, I would love to take your picture.' I was showing him some I've taken before. Right before we left, he was just like, 'Thank you for the music.' And I was like, 'What did somebody tell you? Like, who was talking to you? And literally, what did they say to you?' It was very funny. But he was very kind. He probably has never thought about me again since that time, which is fine.

Did the Braves say anything to you after you released the song?

It's been so weird with the pandemic. I haven't really been as connected as I wish I could have been. But I have been to like three games this season, which still feels really weird, but it's super cool, though.

Did you write the song after meeting him?

No, I've had it written for so long. It almost went on my last record in 2019 but it just didn't feel like the right project for it. I think that's why they let me meet him, because I think somebody said that I had written a song about him. I've never shared it with them. They probably think it's like, 'Yay, go Braves!' And it's not a love song. Maybe if they knew that they would not have let me meet him.

You got to sing "Take Me Out to the Ballgame." I saw the video where you're on the dugout.

Oh my god, how did you see that?

I Googled it.

Is it the real video? Real audio?

It's on someone's phone.

Oh, really? [She pulls up the video] Oh my god I'm watching. Because my dad—oh my god [laughs]. My dad knows one of the people with the Braves—oh my god this is so bad [laughs]. They sent him the Jumbotron video with audio direct from the mic. We have this perfect video, perfect audio. And it is *so* bad [laughs]. I was so nervous. The whole game I'm Googling and just reading the lyrics over and over. And I was like, 'Why am I doing this, everybody knows the lyrics,' but I was so nervous. I thought I was going to forget the lyrics. And then I was like, 'Um, can I go like meet the organ player and make sure we're in the same key?' They were like, 'Okay, that's weird, but okay.' I went up to meet the organ player. The Braves have one of the best organ players I've ever seen in my life. But I went up there and he was just so busy. He was playing and looking at me and talking to me and telling me his schedule while he's just like, fucking smashing this organ [Laughs]. It was so crazy. I was literally screaming into the mic and not singing well at all. There's one point in the song where you say the team name. I didn't know if they're going to say Braves or Bravos so I just pulled the mic really far away. And I was like, making shit up. It's so bad. There's one point in the Jumbotron video where, because I was on top of their dugout, Ronald Acuna Jr. turns around and looks at me, like, 'What the fuck is this horrible music happening right now?' [Laughs]

I want to talk about the music video, it's awesome. What was the idea for it?

I have been working with Matt Swinsky in Atlanta for a while. We've done "Better Distractions" and "Cheers" and all these projects together. I kind of just got to the point where I just really started to trust him. I was like, 'Okay, whenever we do stuff, like, just do it and tell me when to show up, I will be there.' We were kind of like working on treatments together and I really wanted to go to Truist Park and be there during batting practice and be completely ignored by the players. That was my ideal vision—just like, nobody gives a fuck about me because that's kind of what the song is about. But obviously, that was not possible. So we were just like, let's do it *Sandlot* vibes, like whoever wants to be in it can be in it.

So I have to ask you. I'm worried you're going to break my heart right here. The flaming baseball bat. Was that real?

[Long pause] Hey, I don't want to break your heart.

Oh no!

Yeah, it was funny. When we were doing this video, Swinsky would be like, 'Do this, and I know it feels weird, but we're going to edit it in post.' We were so late—like the video was due in two days and comes out in three days. Every scene he's like, 'Don't worry. That's going in post.' We're like, 'Really? Are you sure?' Like there's no real baseballs when we were filming.

I've watched this video a bunch. Do you have shoes with baseball seams on them?
I do. And I used to wear them every day for three years until my friends bullied me to stop wearing them.

They're awesome. What kind of shoes are they?

They're Keds. But they don't make them anymore. Well, they make them now but they're canvas and they're not as cool, but mine were leather. I got my first pair on eBay and wore them until the baseball stitches wore off the shoes. And then I got another pair two years later and wore them for another year until I got bullied out of it. I literally wear those so much.

Do you have a favorite piece of Braves clothing?

Yeah, I have this jersey that I wore when I met [Acuna Jr.]. I randomly got it from the Braves shop. One time I went with somebody who they gave super special attention or whatever, like, they spoiled us. We were on the way out and they were like, 'If you want anything from the shop, it's 75% off for you guys.' And I was like, 'Um, okay, I'll take the $300 jersey and I'll pay not that much, please.' So I've been wearing that a lot. But I have so much vintage Braves stuff that I don't wear anymore. Every time I move it gets its own box.

Last question, and it's one I've thought about many times in my life. What would your walk-up song be?

Hmm. Sometimes I sit at the games and I Shazam walk-up songs. Ozzie [Albies] has some of my favorite walk-up songs because I never know any of them. [Johan] Camargo also has cool walk-up songs. I don't know. I definitely would not choose the Freddie Freeman route, which is just "Eye of the Tiger." [Laughs] Yeah, not doing that. I don't know. It has to be I feel like mine would be something that only hypes me up, like it would literally be a song from *Animal Crossing* or something. It would start playing and people would be like, 'What the fuck?' But I would be like [makes a club beat] walking out getting ready for this shit.

Q: In 2024, Which Atlanta Braves player threw out the first pitch at Faye Webster's concert?
A: Spencer Strider

Illustration by Mark Mosley

Comics

Nobody's Here to See

By Andy Lattimer

IS THERE LESS PRESSURE? OR, IS THERE MORE PRESSURE-
KNOWING THE WORLD WE'RE LIVIING IN-

TO DELIVER?

AND YET,
WITH NO ONE WATCHING,

LUCAS GIOLITO THROWS A NO HITTER.

IT IS AN ACT OF DEFIANCE.
FUCK THE EMPTY FOREST.

IF A MAN ACCOMPLISHES THE UNTHINKABLE IN AN EMPTY STADIUM...
GRANDA 24
THE WORLD GETS A LITTLE BIT EASIER TO LIVE IN.

Baseball Is a Failure-Based Game:
A Comic About Matt Duffy
By Elliot Lin

BASEBALL IS A FAILURE-BASED GAME.

YOU FAIL IN
SO MANY WAYS.
STIIIRKE
DAY IN,
DAY OUT.

YOU UPROOT YOURSELF—
NICE GOING, DUFFMAN!
SAN FRAN

& SAY GOODBYE TO THE TEAM YOU WON WITH.

- CITY THAT HELD YOU
ON ITS SHOULDERS
& LOVED YOU.

YOU MOVE YOURSELF ACROSS THE COUNTRY.
RAYS
YOUR BODY BETRAYS YOU.

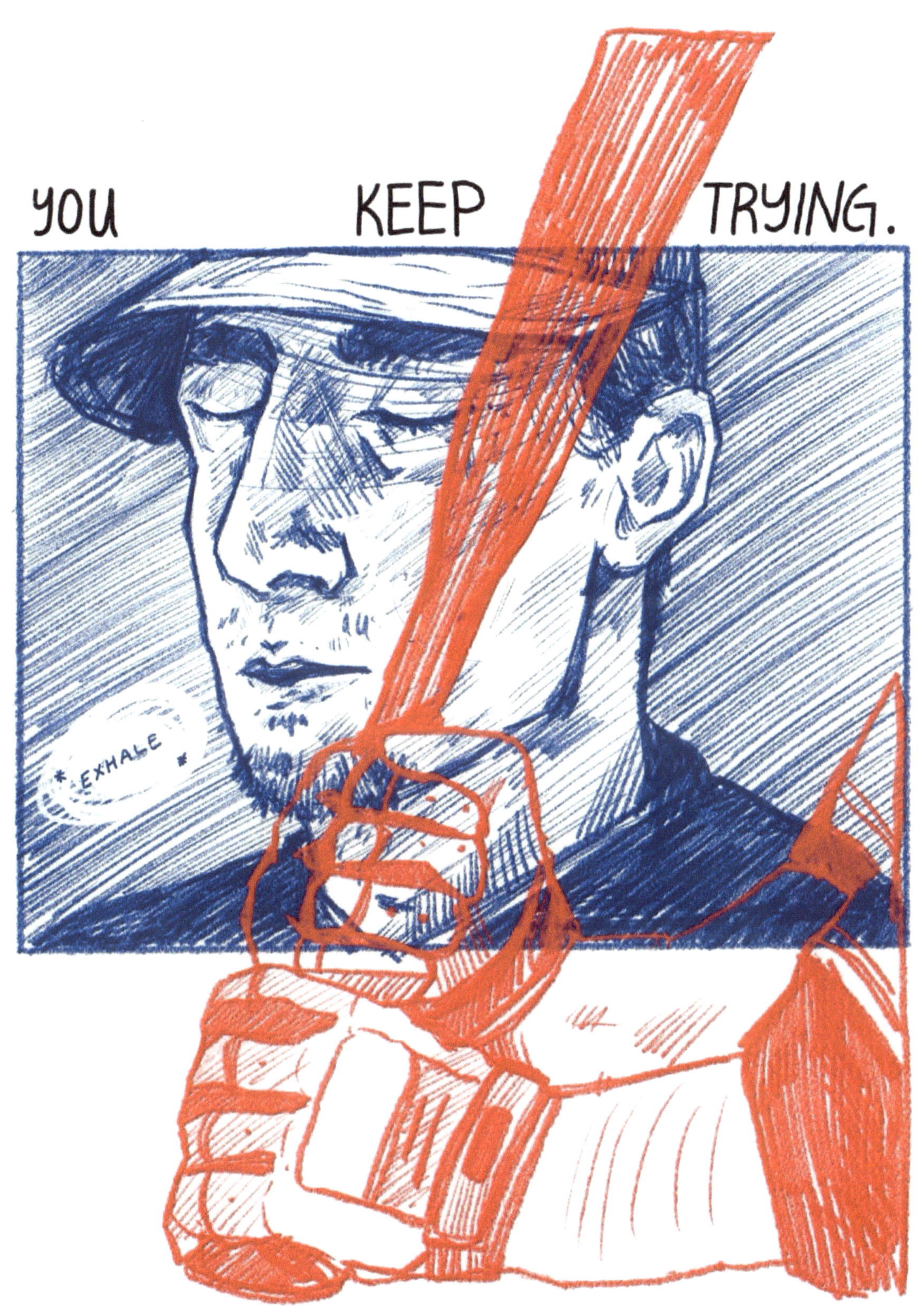

YOU KEEP TRYING.
* EXHALE *

BASEBALL IS A FAILURE-BASED GAME.
YOU TELL YOURSELF,
YOU TELL EVERYONE.

SO IT'S IMPORTANT TO
ALWAYS.
ALWAYS.
ALWAYS.

STAY
POSITIVE!
CUBS
C

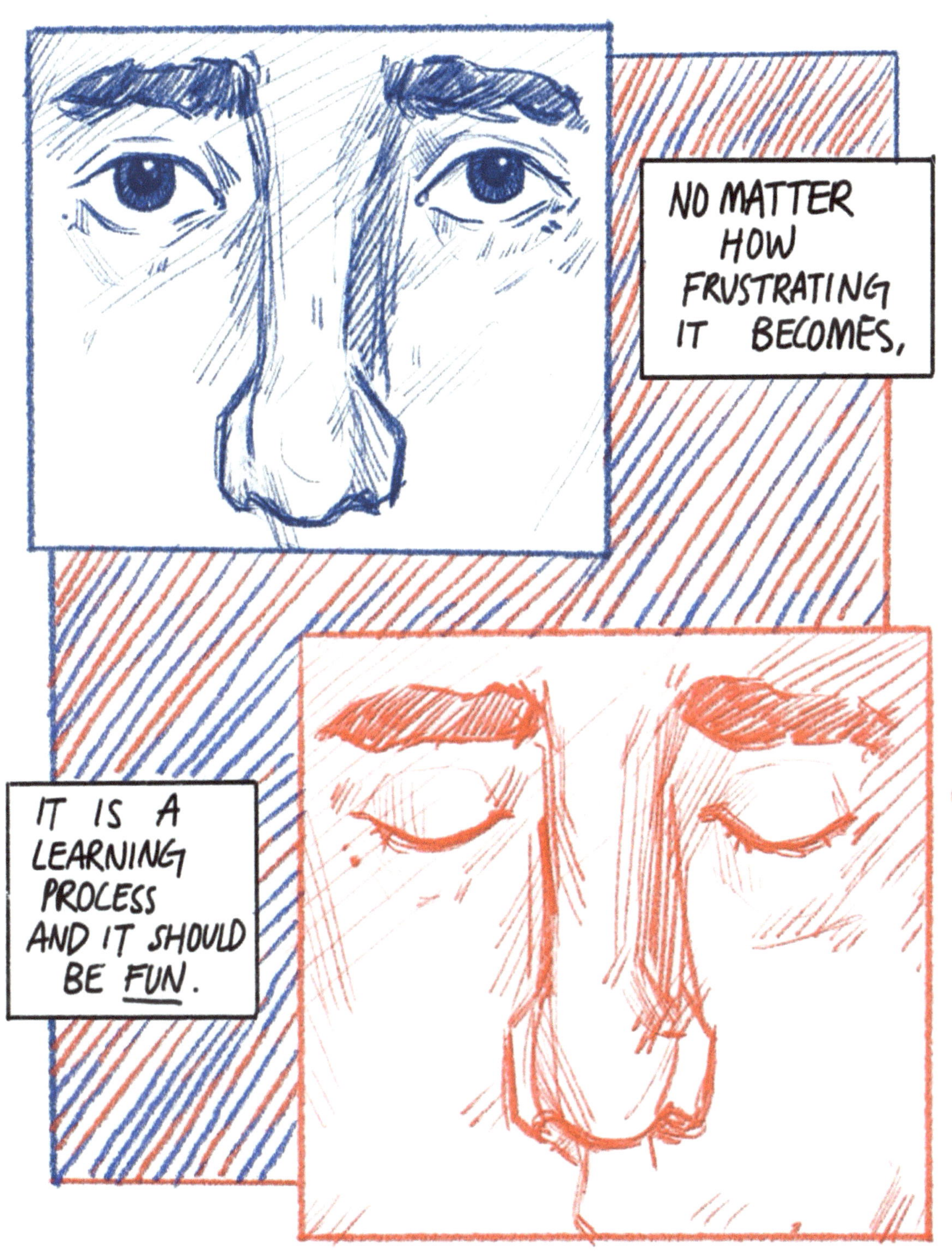

NO MATTER HOW FRUSTRATING IT BECOMES,

IT IS A LEARNING PROCESS AND IT SHOULD BE FUN.

SO. HAVE <u>FUN</u>.

<u>HAVE</u> <u>FUN</u>.

TRUST THAT IF YOU
ENJOY WHAT YOU ARE DOING,
YOU WILL BE MUCH BETTER AT IT.

BASEBALL IS A FAILURE BASED GAME,
BUT THAT SHOULD NOT BE
HOW YOU DEFINE YOURSELF.

Writers

Jack Albert ("BART") is a writer and a baseball fan going back to his Connie Mack Stadium days, sitting in the .75 cent bleachers, watching many future Hall of Famers in their prime. Jack's poetry and prose has been published in a number of sites throughout the years. He attended the Breadloaf School of English at Middlebury College, where in addition to studying American literature, he took Renaissance and Dante courses with Dr. Bartlett Giamatti who later became well-known as Baseball Commissioner.

Ethan Altshul ("The Meaning of Life According to a Groundskeeper") Ethan Altshul is a student at Emory University whose work has appeared in *Rabid Oak, I-70 Review, The Round, Broadkill Review,* and *Evening Street Review.* The grandson of two poets, he currently works as the Executive Editor of *Sophon Lit.* Ethan lives in East Goshen, Pennsylvania, where he is the former Youth Poet Laureate.

Susie Aybar ("The Pursuit of Affirmation Begins, Shea Stadium, 1987") received an MFA from Manhattanville College. Her prose has appeared in *Bright Flash Literary Review, Flash Flood Journal, Tiny Molecules* and is upcoming in *Door is a Jar Literary Magazine.* Her poetry can be found in *ONE ART, The Twin Bill, The San Pedro River Review, Anti-Heroin Chic* and others. She lives in New York and is a lifelong Mets fan. Connect with her at susieaybar.com.

Francois Bereaud ("A Career") is a husband, dad, full time math professor, mentor in the San Diego Congolese refugee community, and mediocre hockey player. He is the author of the collection *San Diego Stories* published by Cowboy Jamboree Press. He has been widely published online and in print. *The Counter Pharma-Terrorist & The Rebound Queen* is his published chapbook. His work has earned Pushcart Best of the Net, and Best Small Fictions nominations. He serves as the fiction editor at *The Twin Bill,* and reads for Porcupine Literary. Links to his writing at francoisbereaud.com.

Nic Bereaud ("A Career") is a former college baseball standout living in San Diego who wants a dog. His current obsession is golf. His father believes he's a latent writer.

Kyle Bilinski ("Last Night at 498") only jacked one home run, in a church league softball game when he was eighteen, and he pumped his fists and jumped up and down as he sprinted around the bases, unable to play it cool. He's written a handful of stories (a poem, too) about slingers and sluggers, which can be found in places like *Hobart* and *Stymie.*

Scott Bolohan ("Duck," interviews with Darryl Strawberry and Faye Webster) is the founder of *The Twin Bill.* His work has appeared in *McSweeney's* and various defunct newspapers. In 2024, he researched the Hank Aaron stamp for the United States Postal Service. He holds a master's in creative writing from the University of Oxford, where he also played baseball as a member of the Oxford Kings, winning the 2016 batting title. He lives in Manhattan where he coaches high school baseball and works as a Yankee Stadium tour guide.

Lindsay Borden ("Glimmering") is a former chef, reformed actor, and late adult-onset Presbyterian pastor. Officially retired, she still gets the almost weekly chance to write and deliver sermons that keep people awake (most of the time). Lindsay lives in New York City where she preaches, volunteers, roots for the Yankees, and writes about the love of God, neighbor, and baseball—not necessarily in that order.

Carey Bowman ("Let's All Get Up") was an aspiring writer and lifelong Cubs fan. Carey's father sent it to *The Twin Bill* after Carey passed at age 28 in 2016.

Clayton Bradshaw-Mittal (they/them) ("Hope in Baseball") writes queer, working-class stories, essays, and poems. Winner of the Plaza Short Story Prize, their creative work can be found in *Story, The Masters Review, Fairy Tale Review, Hole in the Head Review, F(r)iction, South Carolina Review,* and elsewhere. Other writing appears in *The Rumpus, Barrelhouse,* and additional journals. They teach creative writing at Gannon University and are the Managing Editor of *New Ohio Review.*

Loren Broaddus ("Munson") has published a collection of poetry, *Joe DiMaggio Moves Like Liquid Light,* (Andrews-McMeel Press) and two chapbooks, *The Birthing Tree* and *Weight* (Ginkgo Tree Press.) As well as in Twin Bill, his work has appeared in *Spitball: A Literary Baseball Magazine; Turnstyle: The SABR Journal of Baseball Arts;* and in *The Bards of Moon City: an Anthology of Poems.* He spent his childhood rooting for the

Kansas City Royals and his favorite player, Freddie Patek. A U.S. History teacher, he lives in Springfield, Missouri, with his wife and two children. He remains a lifelong baseball fan. lorenbroaddus.com

Mike Cecconi ("The Road to Cooperstown") has been featured in such publications as Utica's Doubly Mad and the UK's Critical Quarterly, receiving honorable mention in the 2020 Wergle Flomp Comedic Poetry Contest. He's performed Rochester Fringe Festival & Manhattan's Anti-Folk Festival as well, part of the TEDx Utica series. He's currently a library aide and runs the Little Falls Public Library's Flash Fiction group. Mike holds a degree in screenwriting from Newhouse at Syracuse & lives in northern New York state. For more, you can follow him on Twitter or watch his TED Talk.

Aarik Danielsen ("Steve Perry Pinch-Hits for Steve Perry") is the arts and culture editor at the Columbia Daily Tribune in Columbia, Missouri. He writes a regular column, The (Dis)content, for *Fathom Magazine*, and has been published at *Image Journal*, *Plough*, *Split Lip*, *HAD*, *Rain Taxi*, *Tinderbox Poetry Journal* and more. Find more of his work at https://aarikdanielsen.com/

Robert Fillman ("The Day that Baseball Taught Third Grade") is a lifelong Mets fan and the author of *The Melting Point* (Broadstone Books, 2025), *House Bird* (Terrapin Books, 2022), and the chapbook, *November Weather Spell* (Main Street Rag, 2019). His poems have appeared in such journals as *Salamander*, *Spoon River Poetry Review*, and *Tar River Poetry*. He teaches at Kutztown University of Pennsylvania.

Jared Frank ("Braves at Phillies, 10/14/22") is a medical writer and Phillies fan residing in Philadelphia. His poetry has previously appeared in *Gargoyle* and *Entropy Magazines*, and his baseball writing in *The Good Phight*. You can follow him on Twitter @JarRFrank.

Cynthia Gallaher ("Grave of the Cracker Jack Boy") is a Chicago-based poet, and author of four poetry collections, including *Epicurean Ecstasy: More Poems About Food, Drink, Herbs and Spices*, and three chapbooks, including *Drenched*. Her award-winning nonfiction/memoir/creativity guide is *Frugal Poets' Guide to Life: How to Live a Poetic Life, Even If You Aren't a Poet*. One of her poems will be sent on NASA's flight to the south pole of the moon later this decade. Gallaher is a lifelong Cubs fan, but will submit to attending White Sox games every so often.

Michael Gaspeny ("Hitting to the Opposite Field") is a retired journalist and teacher living in Greensboro, NC. His most recent books are *Flight Manual: New and Selected Poems* (Unicorn Press) and the novel, *A Postcard from the Delta* (Livingston Press). He's the author of *The Tyranny of Questions,* a novella in verse and two chapbooks. When Gaspeny was a sportswriter in Arkansas, Bob Gibson told him, "You can ask all the questions you like, but I'm not answering any of them." At least the reporter got a brush-off instead of a shave.

Brendan Gillen ("Rickey Henderson Sits by a Lake") is a writer in Brooklyn, NY. His work has been nominated for the Pushcart Prize and Best Small Fictions, and appears in *Electric Lit, Write or Die, Sundog, the Florida Review, Wigleaf, X-R-A-Y*, and elsewhere. His debut novel, *Static*, is available now via Vine Leaves Press. You can find him online at bgillen.com and on Twitter/IG @beegillen.

Matt Gulley ("Two Memories of Miguel Cabrera Two-Run Homers") is a poet, playwright, and fiction writer. He attended Wayne State University in Detroit and currently resides in Brooklyn with his wife Jenna. His work has appeared or is forthcoming in *Quarter After Eight, The Minnesota Review, Consequence Forum, The Madrigal,* and *Moon City Review*. Find him @selfawareroomba on twitter and @mattgulley.bsky.social on Bluesky.

Ruth Hawley ("Ball Mark") has an MFA in Creative Writing at the University of Southern Maine. She is a former collegiate athlete, which informed this piece of flash non-fiction.

Joe Hitchcock ("The Mysterious Yankees Logo") is your friendly neighborhood internet writer. He now lives next door to the Nat Bailey Stadium, home of the Vancouver Canadians, where he spent his summer evenings before COVID.

Terry Horstman ("I need to talk to you about the time Torii Hunter stole a home run from Barry Bonds at the 2002 All-Star Game") is a writer, editor, podcaster, and the all-time lowest scoring player in the history of Minnesota high school boys basketball. A dubious record, but one that can never be broken. His writing has been published or forthcoming by *Flagrant Magazine, Taco Bell Quarterly, The McNeese Review,* and others. He's also the Minnesota Lynx beat writer for *The Next,* and received a 2024 Best of the Net nomination from *The Twin Bill.* He received an MFA in creative writing from Hamline University in 2019 and is a co-founding editor of the sports-themed literary magazine *the Under Review.* Terry lives, writes, and cheers for the Twins in Northeast Minneapolis.

Matthew Johnson ("The Banishment of Moses Fleetwood Walker") is the author of the poetry collections, *Shadow Folks and Soul Songs* (Kelsay Books), *Far from New York State* (NYQ Press), and the chapbook, *Too Short to Box with God* (Finishing Line Press). His work appears / is forthcoming in *The African American Review, London Magazine, Up the Staircase Quarterly,* and elsewhere. He has received recognition and nominations for the Best of the Net, the Pushcart Prize, the Hudson Valley Writers Center, Sundress Publications, and Grand View University. He's the managing editor of *The Portrait of New England.* Originally from Upstate New York and Connecticut, he now lives in North Carolina, rooting for the Yankees and always having his eyes out for the Mets. matthewjohnsonpoetry.com

Paddy Johnston ("The Home Run Jacket, or Learning How to Celebrate") is a writer, musician, comics publisher and podcaster based in Surrey, UK. He is passionate about baseball and promoting baseball in the UK.

Richard Jordan's ("Baseball Haiku") poems appear or are forthcoming in *Southern Poetry Review, Rattle, Terrain, Cider Press Review, Connecticut River Review, Valparaiso Poetry Review, New York Quarterly, Gargoyle Magazine, Tar River Poetry, South Florida Poetry Journal* and elsewhere. His debut chapbook, *The Squannacook at Dawn,* won first place in the 2023 Poetry Box Chapbook Contest. He serves as an Associate Editor for Thimble Literary Magazine.

Amanda Kooser ("Captain Dynamite Will Blow Himself Up") is a freelance journalist specializing in quirky science stories. She graduated from the University of New Mexico creative writing MFA program in 2022. Her work has appeared in *TriQuarterly, Chestnut Review* and *The Saturday Evening Post.* Amanda lives in Albuquerque and plays a pink-sparkle guitar in indie rock band The Dawn Hotel.

Kenny Likis ("The Old Ballgame") grew up in Birmingham, Alabama, watching the Double A Kansas City / Oakland A's play at Rickwood Field. He lives in Cambridge, Massachusetts, taught English at Bunker Hill Community College, collects baseball gloves, and pulls for the Red Sox. His poems have appeared in *Caustic Frolic, Riddled with Arrows, Birmingham Poetry Review,* and *Paterson Literary Review.*

Tim Livingston ("The phanatic") is a poet and a proud Pennsylvanian. They live among friends in Philadelphia with their cat, Mamma Mia!

Eligio Mares ("Oligo My Own") is a wannabe writer, technically just a thinker. He streams down words about the past with hopes they improve the future. He was inspired by a recent trip to the Oligo Nation Gala and Baseball Hall of Fame in New York.

Sara Maurer ("In the Outfield") is a baseball and softball mom who lives and writes in Michigan's Upper Peninsula. While completing the Stanford Continuing Studies novel writing certificate, she wrote her debut novel, *A Good Animal,* which is forthcoming from St. Martin's Press in winter 2026. You can find her at www.saramaurerwrites.com.

Lawrence Miles ("You're Out") is a poet living in White Plains, NY. He has recently been published in *Poets Live Fourth Anthology, 2022 New Generation Beats Anthology,* and *Four Feathers Press' Sounds of Southern California: Poetry of Music.*

Tim Peeler ("Spitballing in the Writing Center") is a retired educator from Western North Carolina who has written twenty-two books of poetry, short stories, and regional history. He has twice been a finalist for the Casey Award for baseball book of the year, and five of his books are housed in the library at the Baseball Hall of Fame in Cooperstown, NY. Most recently he has collaborated with the Appalachian photographer Clayton Young on books that combine verse narratives and rural images.

Linda Petrucelli ("Collector's Item") is a writer obsessed with short form fiction and CNF. Her work has appeared in numerous literary magazines including *Sky Island Journal, Barren, Cagibi, Longridge Review, Permafrost*, and others. Linda's essays have earned Pushcart and Best of the Net nominations. Her story, "Figure Eight on the Waves," won first place in a WOW! Women on Writing Flash Fiction Contest. She lives in Hawaii where she writes and shares a lanai with her baseball card collecting husband, Bonnie the dog, and a passel of cats.

Malavika Praseed ("On Disappearing") Malavika Praseed is a writer, book reviewer, and genetic counselor. She received her MFA from Randolph College in 2025. Her work has appeared in *Khoreo, Bridge Eight, The Twin Bill, Identity Theory, Defunkt, the Chicago Review of Books*, and others.

Travis D. Roberson ("Stadium Rats") is a New York based writer and artist originally from central Florida. His work appears in *The Iowa Review, Cutleaf, Pithead Chapel, Juked*, and many other publications. He is both a Pushcart Prize and Best of the Net nominee, as well as a Porter Fleming Literary Competition winner. He serves as a creative nonfiction Editorial Assistant at CRAFT.

Christopher Rubio-Goldsmith ("Charro Jacket") retired after teaching English for 28 years at a large high school in the middle of Tucson. Now he drinks too much coffee, watches baseball and soccer on the Spanish television stations and goes for long bike rides through the Sonoran Desert. His writings explore growing up in a bilingual/biracial familia. A two-time Pushcart and Best of The Net nominee, his work has recently appeared in *Clockhouse*, the *San Pedro Review* and many other places. He is trying to get better at sitting and seeing. His friends are trying to help.

Paul Ruta ("Just Another Late Inning Go-Ahead Run") is a Canadian currently living in London (no, not Ontario) with a Louisville Slugger signed by Cal Ripken, Jr., and his wife.

Michael Salcman ("Bob From Parkville on the Fan") is a poet, physician and art historian, was former chairman of neurosurgery at the University of Maryland and president of The Contemporary Museum. He is a child of the Holocaust and a survivor of polio. Poems in *Barrow Street, Blue Unicorn, Hopkins Review, Hudson Review, New Letters, Notre Dame Review, Raritan* and *Smartish Pace*. Books include *The Clock Made of Confetti* (nominated for The Poets' Prize), *The Enemy of Good is Better, Poetry in Medicine*, his popular anthology of classic and contemporary poems on doctors, patients, illness, and healing, *A Prague Spring, Before & After* (Sinclair Poetry Prize winner), *Shades & Graces* (winner Daniel Hoffman Legacy Book Prize), *Necessary Speech: New & Selected Poems*, and *Crossing the Tape* (Spuyten Duyvil, 2024).

John Schmidtke ("Camden Yards") lives in Honolulu where he watches MLB.tv at his desk from his office chair while longing to be watching live from the right field bleachers. Family trips to the mainland are planned around seeing a baseball game, majors or minors. Last August he sat in the shade behind the first base dugout and rooted for the home team—the New Hampshire Fisher Cats—as they played the first of a twin bill.

James Scruton ("Night Game: April 8, 2024") has published two collections of poetry and five chapbooks. His baseball poems have appeared over the years in *Spitball, Elysian Fields Quarterly*, and here in *The Twin Bill*, as well as in anthologies of baseball writing.

Jack Smiles ("Major League Dad") is a former community newspaper feature writer collecting short fiction rejections as a hobby in retirement.

AJ Speier-Wallace ("INTERVIEW WITH MY ROTATOR CUFF") is a Black and Jewish college student, outfielder, and Mets fan. When not on the diamond, he is probably writing about it.

Joseph Stanton ("Edward Hoppers Nighthawks Consider the 1942 World Series") has published eight poetry books: *Lifelines: Poems for Winslow Homer and Edward Hopper, Prevailing Winds, Moving Pictures, Things Seen, Imaginary Museum: Poems on Art, A Field Guide to the Wildlife of Suburban Oahu, Cardinal Points: Poems on St. Louis Cardinals Baseball*, and *What the Kite Thinks*. His other books include *Looking for Edward Gorey, The Important Books: Children's Picture Books as Art and Literature*, and *Stan Musial: A Biography*. His poems have appeared in *Poetry, Harvard Review, New Letters, Antioch Review, New York Quarterly, Spitball, Elysian Fields Quarterly, Sport Literate*, and many other journals and anthologies. Articles of his on baseball history, poetry, and art have appeared in issues of *The Cooperstown Symposium on Baseball and American Culture, Nine: A*

Journal of Baseball History & Culture, and *Aethlon: The Journal of Sport Literature.* He is a Professor Emeritus of Art History and American Studies at the University of Hawaii at Manoa.

Carrie Thornbrugh ("The Bases are Loaded and So Are We") is a collector. She collects ideas, memories, rituals, and people and brings them together to create a better version of herself & her community. She has a predilection for the surreal, offbeat, and like the Meatloaf album, *Bat Out of Hell,* she could have been born at any time yet would still be out of place. Her personal loves include DJing, cats, the occult, and her punkmetalfreak baseball team, the Richmond Scrappers.

Barbara Varanka ("Fenway Park") has appeared in *Booth, Moon City Review, Jet Fuel Review, Kawsmouth,* and elsewhere. She lives in Mission, Kansas with her family, and works in software product management. She is a loyal Royals fan, but Fenway Park will always be her favorite place.

Nick Visconti ("Men's league ballplayer") is a writer living in Brooklyn with an artist, and a cat. He plays softball most weekends.

Brendan Walsh ("the iguana is a huge baseball fan") has lived and taught in New England, South Korea, Laos, and South Florida. His work has appeared in Glass Poetry, Rattle, Maine Review, The American Journal of Poetry, and other journals. He is the author of seven collections of poetry, including *concussion fragment,* winner of the 2022 Florida Book Award Gold Medal and *november ninth* (dipity press, 2024). He co-hosts the Fat Guy, Jacked Guy podcast with Stef Rubino, and you can find him online at brendanwalshpoetry.com.

Michael Ward's ("The Errors of Memory") work has appeared most recently in the *Texas Observer, The Tampa Review,* and *The Pinch.* He lives in Dallas with his wife, daughter, and a furry Maltese.

Ken Weisner ("The Thrill of Victory, the Agony of Defeat"), a sidearm pitcher and formerly power-hitting softballista, has published three books with Hummingbird Press, including *Anything on Earth* (2010) and *Cricket to Star* (2019). Ken's latest poetry collection from Shanti Arts is *Songs for the Great Horned* (2024). Editor of *Red Wheelbarrow,* Ken coordinates the annual Red Wheelbarrow Poetry Prize. He asks you to understand that Willie Mays was the greatest of all time.

Shea West (she/her) ("Set Position") lives in Oregon with her family, where she works as a doula and is a volunteer reader for CRAFT. Her work can be read in *Marrow Magazine,* The Twin Bill, and Identity Theory. Much of her work plays with the nuances of wit and suffering and is the joyful product of all the Hamburger Helper she consumed as a child. Her first novel is set to release this spring. You can keep up with her at–www.sheawestauthor.com

Karen J. Weyant ("How to Spit in Little League Baseball") has had poems appear in a variety of publications including *Chautauqua, Crab Orchard Review, Hobart, Lake Effect, New Plains Review, Rattle, Slipstream* and *Whiskey Island.* The author of two poetry chapbooks, her first full-length collection of Poetry, *Avoiding the Rapture,* was published last year by Riot in Your Throat Press. A fan of all underdogs, she loves the Pittsburgh Pirates. She lives, reads, and writes in Warren, Pennsylvania.

Peter Matthiessen Wheelwright ("The Life of Birds") is a novelist, architect, educator (The New School, NYC) and rabid Oriole fan. *As It Is On Earth,* his first novel, received a 2013 PEN/Hemingway Honorable Mention for Literary Excellence. His latest novel, *The Door-Man,* was recognized as one of the "Best Books of 2022" by *The New Yorker.* His uncle is/was three-time National Book Award winner, Peter Matthiessen, who never quite understood his nephew's love for baseball…Go O's. www.peterwheelwright.com

Genoa Wilson ("Myron Noodleman Has a Bad Day") is active with The Downtown Writer's Center in Syracuse NY. Her work has appeared in *Ghost City Review, One Sentence Poems, Women Artists Datebook* and *The Indianapolis Review* among others. She serves as a first reader for *Stone Canoe* and teaches movement for older adults in Central New York. Her poem "Myron Noodleman Has a Bad Day" was nominated by *The Twin Bill* for a best of the net award in 2023.

Dana Yost ("Ruth Talks Hitting") was an award-winning daily newspaper editor and writer for twenty-nine years. Since 2008, he has had nine books published with a tenth forthcoming from Finishing Line Press. He has been nominated for three Pushcart Prizes.

Illustrators

Justine Backlund ("The Mysterious Yankees Logo") is an illustrator and visual art teacher living in Vancouver, Canada.

Mark Bolohan (Faye Webster interview) is an illustrator in the Detroit area.

Jeff Brain ("INTERVIEW WITH MY ROTATOR CUFF") is a San Francisco-based baseball artist and poet. He was a featured poet at the first two National Baseball Poetry Festivals, and now serves on the Poets Committee of the NBPF held each May in Worcester, MA.

Jason David Córdova ("Bob from Parkville on the Fan," "Edward Hopper's Nighthawks Consider the 1942 World Series," "The Old Ballgame," "Charro Jacket," "Captain Dynamite Will Blow Himself Up," "Two Memories of Miguel Cabrera Two-Run Homers" "The Meaning of Life According to a Groundskeeper," "Myron Noodleman Has a Bad Dat," "The phanatic," "Braves at Phillies, 10/14/22," "BART," "Grave of the Cracker Jack Boy," "Set Position," "Steve Perry Pinch-Hits for Steve Perry," "Rickey Henderson Sits by a Lake," Darryl Strawberry interview) lives in Puerto Rico as an illustrator and painter. Some of his art can be seen on Instagram at @jasoni72. You can visit his shop on Red Bubble.

Mike Domina ("The Bases Are Loaded and So Are We") is what you would call a utility player. He's an illustrator, screen printer, visual designer, and web developer drawn towards anything gritty, psychedelic, and rough around the edges. He also plays a mean left-field for the Richmond Scrappers. You can check out his work on Instagram @the_heavy_press.

Gary Robert Hoff ("Collector's Item") is an editorial cartoonist for the *Hawaii Tribune-Herald*, a painter, and teacher who has lived and worked in Hawaii since 2000. His paintings have been exhibited at the Honolulu Academy of the Arts and selected for the Art in Public Spaces program of the Hawaii State Foundation on Culture and the Arts. Hoff taught Visual Arts at Kamehameha High School, Hawaii campus, for 16 years. He lives in North Kohala with his wife, writer Linda Petrucelli.

Andy Lattimer (Poetry illustration, "The Road to Cooperstown," "Last Night at 498," "In the Outfield," "Hope in Baseball," "Nobody Here to See,") is a gay guy making comics about men, real and made up, playing baseball. He also is a freelance illustrator. You can read Andy's most recent work, Safe at Home, an autobiographical comic about COVID-19 and Clayton Kershaw, on his website. His favorite baseball player is Ted Williams, and you can find him on Twitter and Instagram.

Matt Lawrence ("A Career," "Camden Yards," "Glimmering") is a Spanish/ESOL teacher in Baltimore, Maryland. He is the father of two young men and has been deriving joy from making art for decades. You can check out some of his work on Instagram at @Mattymarcador.

Elliot Lin ("The Thrill of Victory, the Agony of Defeat," "I'm Pitching Today," "The Day that Baseball Taught Third Grade," "Ruth Talks Hitting," Creative Nonfiction illustration, "Just Another Late Inning Go-Ahead Run," "On Disappearing," "Oligo My Own," Fiction illustration, "Baseball Is a Failure-Based Game: A Comic About Matt Duffy") is a MA student who spends their free time musing about sports and how they shape or reflect identity, as well as how decision-making and economics influence the world of sports. You can find their other baseball-related illustrations on Twitter @hxvphaestion and Instagram @heph_arts.

Caite McNeil's ("Ball Mark") work can be seen at https://www.caitemcneil.com/

Mark Mosley ("The Banishment of Moses Fleetwood Walker," "Munson," "Spitballing in the Writing Center," "I need to talk to you about the time Torii Hunter stole a home run from Barry Bonds at the 2002 All-Star Game," "Major League Dad") is a public school 7th grade math teacher. He draws baseball cards when he is not driving his son to baseball or his daughter to gymnastics. His cards can be seen on Twitter @mosley_mark, on Instagram @idrawbaseballcards, and can be purchased at https://idrawbaseballcards.bigcartel.com/

Michael C. Paul ("Night Game: April 8, 2024") is an illustrator, writer, and historian. He grew up outside of Kansas City, has moved around a bit over the years working as a history professor, illustrator, and occasionally an editorial cartoonist, and now lives in Northern Virginia with his wife and daughter. For more, visit @MikePaulArt or https://mikepaulart.com.

Michaela Paulson ("the iguana is a huge baseball fan," "The Life of Birds") is an art conservator currently researching the optimal methods for the care and preservation of feathers and feathered cultural heritage materials at the American Museum of Natural History in New York City. She's a novice birdwatcher, learning under the wing(s) of the ornithologists at the museum.

Neon Black Tiger (Interview illustration) is a Portland, OR based artist creating what he calls "Neon Terror" doodles of sports cards, athletes, musicians and anyone else in need of some bright colored craziness. With his use of bright neon colors, snaggletooth fangs and white zombie eyes, Neon Black Tiger certainly stands out in a dollar box. @NEONBLACKTIGER

Tanya Ramsey ("Let's All Get Up") has been working as a professional graphic designer and illustrator for the better part of two decades. Born in Northern Minnesota, Tanya spent most of her life in her home state save for a brief, eight-year stint, in Anchorage, Alaska. Asked why she chose to move back home, she shuddered and replied, merrily, "There were bears." Inspired by classic art movements such as Surrealism and Expressionism, Tanya is also drawn to more recent artists such as Devin Elle Kurtz, the digital artist, iguanamouth, and Omar Rayyan. For more, you can follow her on Bluesky, @dragonnan1.bsky.social or visit her Etsy shop www.etsy.com/shop/JoyCreatingStickers

Travis D. Roberson ("Stadium Rats") is a New York based writer and artist originally from central Florida. His work appears in *The Iowa Review, Cutleaf, Pithead Chapel, Juked,* and many other publications. He is both a Pushcart Prize and Best of the Net nominee, as well as a Porter Fleming Literary Competition winner. He serves as a creative nonfiction Editorial Assistant at CRAFT.

William Scherbarth ("Fenway Park") is six years old. He lives in Birmingham, MI. His biggest inspiration is Jean-Michel Basquiat.

Sam Williams ("Hitting to the Opposite Field," "Baseball Haiku," "Let's Play," "You're Out," "The Pursuit of Affirmation Begins, Shea Stadium, 1987," "Men's league ballplayer," "The Home Run Jacket, or Learning How to Celebrate," "The Errors of Memory," "Duck") is a cartoonist, comics publisher and baseball enthusiast based in Bournemouth, UK.